Achievement for African-American Students

Strategies for the Diverse Classroom

Gary L. Reglin, Ed.D.

National Educational Service
Bloomington, Indiana   1995

Copyright © 1995 by National Educational Service
1252 Loesch Road
Bloomington, Indiana 47404
(812) 336-7700
(888) 763-9045 (toll-free)
FAX: (812) 336-7790
e-mail: nes@nesonline.com
www.nesonline.com

Cover design by Bill Dillon

Printed in the United States of America

Printed on recycled paper

ISBN 1-879639-40-8

With love and thankfulness,

this book is dedicated to my brothers and my sister,

John "Johnny" Reglin, Robert "Bobby" Reglin, and Rena Mae "Rene" Matthews

ABOUT THE AUTHOR

Gary Reglin is tenured Associate Professor of Curriculum and Instruction, University of North Carolina at Charlotte, and Associate Research Scholar/Scientist and Coordinator, Training for Alternative Educators, at the Educational Research and Development Center, University of West Florida, Pensacola.

Dr. Reglin has taught mathematics and managed a successful dropout-retention program in Florida public schools. This program was featured on television and in the February 1990 edition of *Technological Horizons in Education Journal* (T.H.E.). It was also visited by the governor. Reglin's 33 publications are in such refereed journals as the *National Association of Secondary School Principals (NASSP) Bulletin, High School Journal, Middle School League Journal, Journal of At-Risk Issues, Illinois School Journal, The School Administrator, Journal of Computers in Mathematics and Science Teaching,* and the *Journal of Research on Minority Affairs.* He has given presentations at 19 refereed national and state conferences. He has published two books, *Motivating Low-Achieving Students: A Special Focus on Unmotivated and Underachieving African-American Students* and *At-Risk "Parent and Family" Involvement: Strategies for Low-Income Families and African-American Families of Unmotivated and Underachieving Students.* The author is the associate editor of the *Journal of At-Risk Issues* and serves on the editorial board of several journals, including the *Journal of Research on Minority Affairs.* The author teaches "Analysis of Teaching" and "Instructional Design and Evaluation" to preservice educators. He also teaches graduate courses in "Motivating Low-Achieving (At-Risk) Students" and "Effective Parental Involvement and Parental Education Strategies for Educators."

ACKNOWLEDGMENTS

This book, like almost all others, could not have been written without invaluable support from many people. The author wishes to express his gratitude and thanks to all those who gave words of encouragement and assistance as he gathered this information. Special acknowledgment goes to Vermel Moore, 1991-1992 Teacher of the Year from Iredell-Statesville County, North Carolina. Vermel provided many ideas and much information in the preparation of this text.

I would also like to acknowledge the teachers, counselors, dropout-prevention coordinators, and school administrators in summer institutes that I conduct at the University of North Carolina at Charlotte on "Motivating Low-Achieving (At-Risk) Students" and "Effective Parental Involvement and Parental Education Strategies for Educators." These participants critiqued the strategies and models in the book, carefully pointing out what would and would not work for K-12 educators. Excellent suggestions were offered to fill serious gaps in the manuscript.

Paul Lyddon, a graduate student at the University of North Carolina at Charlotte, pursuing a Masters Degree in Teaching English for a Second Language (TESL) devoted many hours in proofreading the manuscript. Paul offered numerous suggestions that are incorporated in this text.

Many colleagues provided significant contributions to Chapter Three. Dr. Peyton Williams, Jr., Associate Superintendent, Office of Instructional Programs, Georgia State Department of Education, made important editorial contributions. Jay Smink (Executive Director), Pat Duttweiler (Assistant Director), and Marty Duckenfield (Public Information Director) of the National Dropout Prevention Center at Clemson University provided critical suggestions that greatly enhanced the strategies suggested in Chapter Three. Dr. Alex Martinez, principal of Rio Vista Elementary School in Tucson, Arizona, completed a thorough review of the manuscript. His suggestions led to significant changes in Chapter Four. Dr. Ann Reitzammer, Editor of *The Journal of At-Risk Issues,* critiqued the manuscript and added many valuable ideas.

I wish to express my gratitude and thanks to three significant persons that have given me considerable encouragement and strength throughout my adult life, without which none of my accomplishments would be possible. These important people are my loving sister, Rena Mae Matthews; brother John "Johnny" Reglin; and my brother Robert "Bobby" Reglin. Lastly, this book was supported in part by a grant from the foundation of the University of North Carolina at Charlotte and the State of North Carolina.

TABLE OF CONTENTS

Table of Contents (continued)

FOREWORD

Schools are not succeeding with our current generation of African-American students. In far too many minority communities, schools simply fail to provide the quality of education needed to sustain the hopes, dreams, and aspirations of young African-Americans. The data—dropout rates, marginal achievement test scores, disruptive school behavior, low student self-esteem, and poor college attendance—all indicate that a vast segment of these students are being underserved by their schools.

As educators finish this decade and contemplate the start of a new millennium, the teaching of minority, low-income, and underprivileged students will remain a central theme in education discussions. While society has generally embraced a changed attitude about the role of education for African-American students, some sobering questions must be addressed if all students are to receive the educational benefits and privileges currently provided to the most fortunate:

1. Who will successfully teach America's children, particularly African-Americans?

2. Is there a need for comprehensive school policies designed to strengthen the cultural consciousness and intercultural competence of the teaching force?

3. What attitudes and skills will teachers need to reach their socioeconomically disadvantaged students, particularly African-Americans?

4. What instructional practices are most advantageous in classrooms where African-American students are the majority enrollment?

5. Can we as a nation afford to underserve our minority students?

Dr. Reglin is to be commended for pursuing the research needed to address these questions. *Achievement for African-American Students* provides pre- and in-service K-12 educators with the valuable answers they need to achieve success with their increasingly diverse students. These strategies are essential in communities where there are relatively high enrollments of African-American students. Educators will find that *Achievement for African-American Students*:

- Provides teachers with instructional strategies designed to help them interact more positively with learners from diverse ethnic and racial backgrounds

- Identifies effective means of empowering African-American males for successful school achievement

- Describes measures that will greatly increase the involvement of African-American parents in the education of their children

- Suggests ways to teach classes, manage classrooms, and interact with students so that the educational desires of all learners are stimulated and nurtured

- Provides strategies for motivating urban African-American students toward success at school and in life.

The commitment to increasing minority student achievement is a responsibility communities must not abdicate. But in order for teachers to educate well, they must be fully cognizant of the various cultural milieus, diverse value systems, assumptions about education, and socio-cultural life patterns that connect diverse learners to the home, school, and community. Dr. Reglin provides teachers with ample resources to make these connections a reality. I recommend Dr. Reglin's book as a resource teachers *must* use to achieve greater success in working with African-American learners and their families.

Howard D. Hill, Ph.D.
Director of Chapter Programs
Phi Delta Kappa
Adjunct Professor of Afro-American Studies
Indiana University/Bloomington

PREFACE

A disproportionate number of urban African-American students, especially males, are failing to meet the expectations of public schools. By not meeting these expectations, the students may feel inadequate and drop out. Lacking the skills needed to productively participate in today's society, many are destined to lives of poverty and despair. Perhaps we need to ask ourselves, "Are the students failing the system or is the system failing the students?"

Teachers often report that they were not taught the skills necessary to work effectively with African-American students. Gary Reglin has done an outstanding job in providing a very timely and much needed text which provides teachers with approaches for helping African-American students succeed in school and in life. Dr. Reglin's expertise in the at-risk arena is evident as he conveys an awareness that could only come from one who is committed to making a difference for students who are in at-risk situations. His text details initiatives for restructuring education and attitudes which result in a more sensitive, caring environment for African-American students. It also describes measures which will increase the involvement of parents or guardians.

Achievement for African-American Students: Strategies for the Diverse Classroom will be helpful to teachers from all walks of life. The recommendations in this text will help teachers to understand the needs of their African-American students and to motivate them to realize the highest levels of accomplishment. Teachers have the responsibility to help students experience success and to become life-long learners.

I invite you to read *Achievement for African-American Students: Strategies for the Diverse Classroom.*

> *Ann F. Reitzammer*
> *Editor, The Journal of At-Risk Issues*
> *Executive Board Member*
> *The National Dropout Prevention Network*
> *Associate Professor, Huntingdon College*

INTRODUCTION

This book was designed to provide teachers of grades kindergarten to twelve (K-12) with techniques and approaches for helping their many urban African-American students achieve and succeed in school. In many places, a disproportionate number of these children—particularly African-American males—are failing to meet the demands and expectations of our public school systems. This book contains suggestions for strategies and approaches that work effectively with this ethnic minority that teachers find difficult to deal with. Educators will find the book an excellent supplementary text for a multicultural course such as "Teaching in an Urban Society."

This work presents a planned approach to four major initiatives: (1) to restructure the instruction and behaviors commonly practiced in most classrooms today; (2) to provide teachers with approaches and strategies that will help them interact more positively with their multicultural students; (3) to provide social and instructional strategies specifically designed for effectiveness with African-American male students; and (4) to describe a series of measures that will greatly increase African-American parents' involvement in their children's education. These initiatives will help teachers restructure their instruction and behaviors so that they are more sensitive to ethnic minorities, particularly African-Americans. Restructuring instruction and behaviors means modifying the strategies used to teach classes, manage classrooms, and interact with students so that the learning needs of all students are met. Such restructuring of instruction and behaviors is especially needed to make African-American students feel that the school is their place.

The strategies in this book will be helpful to all teachers, public or private, rural or urban, from whatever racial or ethnic background. Approximately 90 percent of teachers are from the majority Anglo-American culture, and 72 percent of them are female. These majority-culture female teachers will find the plans and suggestions in this work particularly useful. The book is also useful for middle-class African-American teachers, many of whom grew up in predominantly Anglo-American communities, attended predominantly Anglo-American private high schools, and graduated from predominantly Anglo-American universities.

Why does a book on multicultural education focus particularly on one ethnic minority group, African-Americans? In all of the many workshops that I have conducted on the East Coast in the last five years, the number one concern K-12 teachers have shared with me has been their difficulty in motivating African-American students to achieve and behave appropriately in the classroom. Even after the workshops were over, majority- and minority-culture teachers would remain behind to show me the low achievement scores of their African-American students and to talk about their many discipline problems. Urban public-school principals tell me that they are desperate for inservice help to assist teachers to deal effectively with their African-American students.

In my county, Charlotte-Mecklenburg, Superintendent John Murphy has made a priority of bridging the wide gap in achievement between the African-American students and all other ethnic groups. For a number of years, African-Americans have had the lowest achievement and the highest number of discipline referrals of any ethnic minority group in the Charlotte-Mecklenburg public school system. The problems in this school district are typical of many other large urban districts. By developing a plan for multicultural teaching based on the experience of one school system with one ethnic minority group, I am hoping to stimulate other scholars to develop similar books on ethnic-minority groups that the system is failing, such as the Hispanic-Americans and the Native Americans.

I have organized my suggestions for new approaches and teaching innovations into four chapters.

Chapter One tells why we cannot continue to do "business as usual" in our schools and why we need new and innovative teaching strategies. When teachers properly implement instruction and supportive teaching behaviors that are sensitive to ethnic minorities—especially African-Americans—they will be molding an innovative instructional system. K-12 educators will soon come to three major understandings: that the hidden and implicit "null curriculum" exerts tremendous power on classroom dynamics; that practicing instruction and behaviors sensitive to ethnic minorities is an ongoing process; and that such instruction and behaviors are multidimensional.

After discussion of the "self-fulfilling prophecy" and importance of conveying high but realistic expectations, Chapter One presents several models for questionnaires and checklists. The Ethnic-Minority-Attitude Interview Questionnaire (EMAIQ) is a model for the kinds of questions administrators can use to gauge the attitudes and willingness of prospective teachers to pursue encounters with the families and community of their prospective multicultural students. The Ethnic-Minority-Sensitive Expectations Checklist (EMSEC) helps teachers, working with an observer or mentor, appraise the kinds of expectations they communicate to their African-American students. To ensure that teachers, whether of the majority or minority culture, do not implicitly imply the superiority of any one culture over another, the chapter includes a set of discussion and reflection questions, the Ethnic-Minority-Sensitive Respect Model (EMSRM).

Chapter One concludes by showing that genuine innovation empowers teachers as they develop awareness of other cultures. The four workshop activities suggested in the Ethnic-Minority-Sensitive Awareness Activities (EMSAA) lead educators to develop an awareness and understanding of terms and statements sensitive to ethnic minorities.

Chapter Two contends that teaching must be restructured to support instruction and behaviors that are sensitive to ethnic minorities. Activities that promote this endeavor are described:

- planning lessons inclusive of African-American culture
- planning lessons that capitalize on African-American students' interests

- planning cooperative-learning (CL) activities
- teaching social skills
- understanding the effect of school and class climate
- modeling caring
- modeling attitudes and behaviors that reduce a chilly school climate
- assessing the school and classroom climate
- implementing initiatives to enhance a more positive climate
- assessing the media for stereotyping
- resolving conflicts arising from ethnic differences
- organizing a portfolio of interactions with African-Americans

The Ethnic-Minority-Sensitive Lesson Plan (EMSLP), presented in Chapter Two, is a useful model for a three-component lesson-design plan for urban classrooms with a large number of African-American students who are failing academically. Teachers are encouraged to work with mentors to implement this lesson plan. Its first component (Daily Lesson Plan Outline) is used to develop a lesson plan. Component II (Ethnic-Minority-Sensitive Checklist) can be employed in reviewing the lesson plan to ensure its sensitivity to the needs of the African-American students. Component III (Reflections on Strengths and Weakness), to be completed after the lesson has been taught, helps the teacher evaluate its strengths and weakness.

Many unmotivated and underachieving African-American students do not understand or respond to lesson activities that make little connection to their interests and experiences. To remove this barrier to their success, the three Ethnic-Minority Classroom Interest Inventories (EMCIIs) in Chapter Two (designed for different grade levels) integrate African-American students' interests and experiences into the lesson plan. The list of Ethnic-Minority-Sensitive Cooperative-Learning Activities (EMSCLA) provides a model for helping educators, individually or in inservice workshops, work effectively with African-American students. These activities can be used with the Ethnic-Minority-Sensitive Cooperative Checklist (EMSCC), a model of the kinds of approaches and strategies to consider when designing and implementing an effective cooperative-learning activity.

Many urban African-Americans from impoverished backgrounds come into the classroom lacking social skills, which must be taught to them. The climate in many schools reflects middle-class Anglo-American culture and values. African-American students need to perceive that the classroom climate is not foreign to them and that it is one in which they can feel secure from public embarrassment and criticism. The steps listed in the Ethnic-Minority Climate-Building Initiatives (EMCBI) assist teachers in molding a warm and supportive classroom and school climate.

Even after beginning climate-enhancing initiatives, a teacher cannot automatically assume that all African-American students will perceive the classroom climate as being warm and supportive. Educators can assess the climate and their progress in improving it by asking questions, observing African-American students for signs of dissatisfaction, and administering classroom-climate surveys to all students four times a year. Chapter Two provides three Classroom-Climate Inventories (CCIs) for conducting such surveys.

Teachers often need to be coached to make positive statements about African-American students when they are in the classroom. It is also important to make these statements in the presence of adults in such locations as in the teachers' lounge, cafeteria, and at faculty meetings. Examples of positive statements and affective climate-enhancing quotations are discussed. Chapter Two concludes with strategies both for the prevention of African-American stereotyping and for effective conflict resolution.

In my workshops for public-school educators at all grade levels, majority-culture teachers and middle-class African-American teachers expressed frustration over an inability to teach and deal effectively with the subcultures of urban African-American male students. Numerous African-American males are not being adequately served by the public schools. They are disciplined, expelled, and suspended at higher rates than any other group.

Chapter Three delineates a blueprint for action to promote more positive interactions between teachers and their African-American male students in order to engender and reinforce these students' experiences of success. A major goal of the action plan is to have the students so pleased and occupied with successful experiences and the good feeling these engender that any attention-seeking, ego-satisfying misbehaviors will rapidly disappear. Examples of innovative activities and strategies are organized into six areas:

- dealing with African-American male subculture ("cool posing")
- dealing with racism and perceptions of victimization
- emphasizing the whole child
- building self-esteem
- cross-age and peer tutoring
- learning-styles instruction

Chapter Four seeks to challenge the myth that urban African-American parents do not want to get involved in school, a myth that is prevalent in public-school education. Research supports my personal experience that all parents care about the education of their children. Innovative strategies to augment the involvement of African-American parents are presented. Many families feel a sense of isolation, intimidation, and powerlessness as they relate to the schooling and education of their children. Techniques to make the school user-friendly to the families are outlined.

Chapter Four concludes with a discussion of two vital initiatives to increase parental involvement. The first is a set of programs and strategies to improve the home-school-community connections; the second approach is an innovative strategy to get the community to supply positive role models for African-American children.

I hope that readers will find this book as helpful and practical as it was intended to be. I have attempted to be as brief and straightforward as possible. My wish is to contribute to the continuing effort to restructure our K-12 instructional strategies and activities so that the educational experiences of all children will be more meaningful, enjoyable, and productive. The suggestions in this text should help teachers motivate their urban African-American students to reach the high achievement levels that are well within their grasp.

CHAPTER

Restructuring Instruction and Behaviors

Chapter One Objectives

After reading this chapter, readers should be able to:

Explain what it means to restructure instruction and behaviors for multicultural students, especially urban African-Americans.

Discuss why it is important to use innovative strategies when teaching urban African-Americans and other multicultural students.

Discuss three important areas of innovation that teachers can focus on when teaching urban African-American students.

Identify the function of four models of plans or activities that can help restructure instruction and behaviors to be more effective with urban African-American students. The models include the

Ethnic-Minority-Attitude Interview Questionnaire

Ethnic-Minority-Sensitive Expectations Checklist

Ethnic-Minority-Sensitive Respect Model

Ethnic-Minority-Sensitive Awareness Activities

The scene is any city high school, USA. Miss Moore, a young first-year teacher who is deter-mined to help her ninth-grade "at-risk" students, is seated at her desk, planning her first-period class. The bell rings and the sudden uproar in the halls announces the students' arrival. Malcolm, a 15-year-old African-American, is one of the first through the door. He's surrounded by five or six of his close friends.

Malcolm approaches Miss Moore's desk to turn in a homework assignment. He's been a quiet student so far, not contributing anything to the class but not causing any trouble either. Although he has been doing his work, it is often hasty and careless. Miss Moore believes he can do better, and she wants to motivate him to achieve. She looks up at him.

Malcolm is a large boy, probably weighing 40 pounds more than his teacher. His cap is turned backwards. His T-shirt, over-large even on his broad shoulders, displays the face of Malcolm X, a clenched fist, and a defiant slogan. His baggy pants hang low on his hips, revealing a couple of inches of his undershorts. Most of his friends are dressed similarly.

"Malcolm," says Miss Moore, "you know those clothes are not appropriate for school. Surely your parents don't want you to dress like that. What would happen if you went to a job interview looking the way you do now?"

Malcolm freezes a few steps from her desk. The clamor in the room gives way to sudden silence. All the students are watching the two of them. Malcolm scowls and draws himself up taller. His movement jangles the gold chains he is wearing.

Miss Moore realizes that Malcolm is indeed very large—quite intimidating, in fact—but she is determined to continue. "All those gold chains," she says. "I can't believe your parents can afford to have all their money put into your jewelry."

At that moment, Touré, one of Malcolm's closest friends, shouts tauntingly from the back of the room, "His parents don't care. With all they make dealin' drugs, Malcolm can buy what-ever he wants!"

After a moment of shocked silence, it's bedlam in the room. Malcolm's and Touré's friends shout and jeer. "Tell her, man, tell her the way it is!" Other students look frightened.

Malcolm looks at his friends and then turns back to his teacher. "Miss Moore," he says icily, "there are people in this world who are not like you. What's it to you anyway what I wear in school?" He mutters something that sounds very much like an obscenity to Miss Moore.

Miss Moore can see her control of the classroom slipping away quickly. She is beginning to cry. "You do not speak to your teachers like that," she says, reaching for her pad of pass slips and discipline referrals. "I want you to report to the assistant principal immediately."

Malcolm angrily snatches the slips off her desk. "I'll go," he says, "but I won't be comin' back. I'm outta this dump."

He storms from the room, on his way to becoming another school dropout.

An incident like this could happen in almost any school in the United States. Teachers are frustrated by what they perceive as minority students' sullen rejection of their efforts to help them and by their continuing low achievement and disruptive behavior. The students are equally turned off by what they sense as a lack of respect for them and their culture and the total irrelevance of everything that goes on in the classroom to their lives.

We can turn around this continuing deterioration in the educational situation of minority youth—especially African-American males—and their increasing alienation from all that our schools currently offer them. To do so, however, will require a total reversal of many of our traditional instructional practices and a massive change in the social climate that prevails in most of our schools.

We cannot continue to do business as usual.

THE NEED FOR RESTRUCTURED INSTRUCTION AND BEHAVIORS

NO MORE BUSINESS AS USUAL

In many public schools, a large number of urban African-American children are failing to achieve academic success. We must heed the calling not to do business as usual for these youth. When African-American students don't experience academic success in school, the consequence may be delinquent behavior, both at school and in society at large.

Public-school systems are using hand-held metal detectors. Administrators regularly conduct random searches in junior- and senior-high classrooms. Uniformed police officers patrol middle and high schools. Drug- and weapon-sniffing dogs are common in schools. Cameras are installed on school buses. These measures are prevalent throughout the nation in urban schools with substantial numbers of African-American students.

Safety has become a major concern of urban public-school teachers. Nationally, my colleagues say that it is becoming a daily battle to motivate urban teachers of grades kindergarten to twelve (K-12) to remain in the profession. Needless to say, some fear for their lives. Most do not feel properly trained to deal with the problems of African-American students.

In a brainstorming session for solutions, a high-school principal said, "The enemy that we are trying to stop is a feeling of hopelessness and despair, the enemy of being a victim.... We don't know how to love, care, build meaningful positive relationships, and forgive anymore. Metal detectors and cameras do not detect and cannot prevent the feelings of hopelessness and despair in many of our children."

When one investigates the perpetrators of many of today's acts of violence, a disproportionate number are young, misguided, urban African-American students. All students can succeed in school and in life if they are adequately served by society, government, the community, their families, and the public schools. Building more prisons is not the solution to underachievement, crime, and violence. The ultimate solution rests on the shoulders of K-12 teachers, who can help students—especially urban African-Americans—experience the meaning of success during their early school years and who can promote their opportunities for successes throughout the public-school years.

Comer (1987) found that many unmotivated and underachieving urban African-American students are turned off to life and to school. The students feel they have no stake in the school. There is no sense of ownership. They can perform adequately in the housing project, in the trailer parks, on the playground, and in a variety of other places, but not in school. Comer found that many of the teachers respond to these children by controlling or attempting to control them, or by having low expectations of them. This has caused the students either not to respond or to respond in ways that made matters worse.

When I write about restructuring instruction and behaviors, I am thinking of the need to modify the strategies used to teach classes, manage classrooms, and interact with students so that the learning needs of *all* students are met. Such measures can make African-American students feel that the school is their place. This kind of restructuring seeks to identify creative, new, and effective ways of organizing and delivering educational services (Jenks, 1988). Such restructuring in grades K-12 will help teachers plan and deliver instruction and model behaviors that are sensitive to the needs of African-American students. Restructuring will train and encourage K-12 educators not to do business as usual, but to innovate. Restructuring must be an important part of our school reformation process.

A DIRE NEED TO INNOVATE

Tradition is a valuable and comforting source of stability, but sometimes tradition no longer serves. When the demands made on classroom teachers change, the way classroom teachers prepare for them must also change (Reglin, 1990). Innovation means questioning every aspect of teaching and learning. It means looking beyond what is and envisioning what could be.

Innovation means teachers molding an instructional system that capitalizes on the strengths inherent in properly implementing instruction and teaching behaviors sensitive to the needs of African-American youth. Why is it important to innovate? Innovation is crucial to enhancing the academic motivation of numerous uninspired and failing African-American students. Innovation will help teachers confront the challenge of educating urban African-American students.

In a mere 10 years, fully one-third of all public-school pupils will be minority students, according to the Commission on Minority Participation in Education and American Life (Banks, 1989). In 30 years, more than 40 percent of the total American population will consist of minorities.

The face of the American workforce will change dramatically in the next century. Minorities will constitute a disproportionate share of the workforce. Native-born Anglo-American males will make up only 15 percent of the new entrants to the labor force during this period (Johnson & Packer, 1987). One-third of the workers will be minorities.

The current school-enrollment picture reveals that in 23 of the nation's 25 largest cities, minorities constitute the majority of students. In 1971, 11.7 percent of the teachers were minorities. In 1986, 10.3 percent were minorities (Nicklos & Brown, 1989).

The trend is clear: the proportion of already under-represented African-American teachers is declining. A recent survey (Daniels, 1989) found that 41 percent of the African-American teachers surveyed said they would probably leave teaching in the next five years, compared to 25 percent of the White teachers. Increasingly, then, majority-culture teachers will be called upon to innovate and teach groups of so-called African-American-culture students. As a starting point in the innovation process, teachers can reflect seriously in three important areas: (1) understanding and employing the "null" or hidden curriculum effectively; (2) creating supportive and welcoming classroom climates; and (3) infusing all instruction with a multidimensional, multicultural component.

First, it is important to understand how to employ the null curriculum effectively. The null curriculum is defined as the hidden, implicit curriculum, embedded in the culture of the classroom and the school. This hidden curriculum serves to socialize youth to particular norms and values. Before- and after-school time affords excellent opportunities for capitalizing on the null curriculum. Understanding and utilizing this concept are significant in the school success of African-American students. As Eisner (1985) reminds us, the null curriculum (what schools do not teach explicitly) has important effects on the successes and failures of all school children.

Rules, procedures, behaviors, interactions with students, interactions with all adults, and the taken-for-granted classroom and school processes can be critically examined to ascertain the impact on the null curriculum. All should be examined to see if they support diversity in the classroom (O'Connor, 1989).

Silent, often unintended objectives embedded in educational methods and processes can have detrimental effects on classroom interactions and African-American student learning (Banks, 1993a). School innovations can influence students in different ways. Delpit (1988) demonstrated this in her writings on an African-American student who became upset with an Anglo-American professor using a process approach to teach writing. The student did not believe the teacher was making an effort to teach the class. The process approach was more culturally congruent with the mainstream Anglo-American students than it was for the African-American students. Instructional innovations that emphasize process rather than the direct teaching of skills can be harmful to students who equate a lack of structure with a lack of caring. Urban educators are more effective in dealing with African-American students when they are cognizant of the rationale underlying the null curriculum and its power in teaching and learning.

Second, teachers can view innovation in instruction and behaviors in education as steps toward creating a classroom environment that is more nurturing toward disaffected minority students. A paramount component of this process is to promote daily reflection on some important questions:

> • Is my classroom climate warm and supportive for African-American students who do not participate in class discussions and who are consistently failing my exams?

• Is my classroom inviting for all students?

• Is there a significant emphasis on cooperative activities as opposed to competitive activities?

• Are students cooperating on written take-home examinations, working in cooperative-learning groups for class projects, and working on practice/reinforcement activities cooperatively instead of independently?

• Are my African-American students repeatedly ending up as losers instead of winners?

• Is my teaching style supportive of the learning styles of African-American students?

• Do I voice my dissatisfaction when the school tracks African-American students into remedial courses, non-marketable vocational skills, and low-paying/low-status jobs?

Reflecting on these challenging questions when working with African-American students will lead to better lessons and better interactions with the students. More achievement will be evident. Misbehaviors in class and in society will be reduced. Successful students will feel good about themselves and will concentrate on good behaviors instead of bad behaviors.

Teachers who begin to view instruction and behaviors as a process of continuing improvements may need to be prepared for an uphill battle. In many schools, the curriculum is much the same today as it was during the time of the Civil War (Valverde, 1993). The program is more varied and the list of offerings more extensive, but for all practical purposes the focus has remained the same. The planning and teaching have tended to have a monocultural thrust that reflects majority middle-class Anglo-American culture, which has been transmitted to all learners. Curriculum materials, instructional strategies, and teaching behaviors are likely to reflect the majority culture.

Many schools have continued to present one set of values, one type of lifestyle, and one mode of behavior, and they have expected African-American students to accept these. In such cases, curriculum restructuring is essential if the school is to move from a monocultural approach to a multicultural one that will meet the cultural needs of all students. Curriculum restructuring must include input from African-American students, African-American communities, and African-American businesses. When this is done, the schools can be effective in transmitting effective instruction and behaviors to all learners.

Urban African-American families must be significant players in restructuring efforts. Many will help if teachers and administrators are creative and offer a properly extended invitation. Such an invitation requires more than a memo or phone call. Bold and aggressive measures may be required to overcome the deep distrust of the public schools held by many urban African-Americans. It can make a real difference when educators visit churches, community centers, grocery stores, beauty shops, barber shops, and other places in the African-American communities where African-Americans tend to congregate, in order to invite them into the school. Teachers have used the school bus to travel to the homes of their students, and they have invited parents to get on the bus to go to meetings at the school. Educators can anticipate the complaints of parents that they recently left work and did not have time to eat by making pizza and soft drinks available during the parent meeting at the school. Funds from the Parent-Teacher-

Student Organization (PTSO) may be available to purchase the pizza, and soft drink distributors may be willing to contribute the beverages.

To increase PTSO participation, schools should put on a short play at meetings, with roles rotated so that many of the African-American children will be involved at one time or another. Parents enjoy seeing their children perform on stage. This innovative technique will cause more parents to attend traditional meetings. Some teachers and tutors have gone into the public housing community's self-service laundry during the evenings to help children with their homework. They found that many middle-school children washed clothes for their families on Tuesdays and Fridays, so there were many children and parents in the laundry on these days. This turned out to be an excellent opportunity to tutor children for two hours and to communicate with parents.

Third, I concur with Banks, Shade, and other experts who say that teachers need to view instruction and behaviors multidimensionally. One problem that continues to plague the multi-cultural-education movement, both from within and without, is the tendency of teachers, administrators, policy makers, and the public to oversimplify the concept (Banks, 1993b). Culturally sensitive instruction and behaviors are complex and multidimensional concepts that are applicable to all courses, students, and educators. One dimension is the extent to which teachers use examples, data, and information from a variety of cultures and groups to illustrate important concepts, rules, and procedures in their subject areas or discipline. An example would be using biographies of African-American mathematicians and famous African-American writers in mathematics and English.

Another dimension involves discussion of the ways in which the implicit cultural assumptions and biases within a discipline influence the formulation of knowledge. This dimension helps students understand how knowledge is created and how it is influenced by factors of race, ethnicity, and social class. Concepts, explanations, and interpretations that African-American students derive from personal experiences in their homes, families, and cultures must be explored. This perspective is vital to preclude classroom cultural conflict. Cultural conflict occurs in the classroom because much of the personal/cultural knowledge that the urban African-American students bring to the classroom is inconsistent with school knowledge and with teachers' personal and cultural knowledge.

A third dimension is pointing out to students that the knowledge that is institutionalized by the mass media and other forces that shape the popular culture has a strong influence on the values, perceptions, and behaviors of children. The messages and images carried by the media often reinforce the stereotypes and misconceptions about African-Americans that are institutionalized within the larger society. By the age of four, African-American children are aware of racial differences and show racial preferences favoring Anglo-Americans (Banks, 1993b).

In restructured classrooms, all students can be helped to develop more positive racial attitudes if realistic images of African-American groups are included in teaching materials and students work in ethnically mixed cooperative-learning groups designed to help them to develop more positive racial attitudes and behaviors (Shade, 1989). Teachers must not only sensitize attitudes but build high expectations, promote respect, and foster an awareness of African-American youth and families' culture and unique obstacles.

My personal experiences support research that shows that more multicultural innovations need to exist in a great many K-12 classrooms. Better and different strategies should be available to teachers to prepare them to deal adequately with African-American students. Yet, for the most part, business is being conducted as usual.

MENTORING AND INSERVICE WORKSHOPS TO DEVELOP SENSITIVE ATTITUDES

Mentor teachers and inservice workshops are excellent ways to facilitate teachers' reflection on the attitudes they project in their day-to-day interactions with African-American students. Both can facilitate development of a sense of genuine empathy for African-American children in and outside the classroom. One effective strategy is to have teachers design role-playing activities to place themselves in the shoes of African-American students so that the teachers can experience the myriad and varied obstacles these students face in the community and in the school. Teachers will realize that the transition from home to school may be a difficult one for the urban African-American child. The students' values, preparation, and experiences are somewhat different from those taught in school. The following students are representative of many underachieving African-American students in the public schools:

(1) Jamal is from a family too proud to ask for public assistance;

(2) Aumi is pregnant and has not told her mother. Her mother will be very angry; and

(3) Keito is being raised by a single parent after a traumatic divorce involving physical abuse and alcoholism.

No matter how much these students want to succeed, life's problems are overwhelming.

Early positive experiences with African-American parents shape positive attitudes in teachers. Frequent interactions and visits with parents by educators will allow them to become more sensitized to life on the other side of the fence and to perceive the African-American parent as a concerned educational partner. Teachers might be coached to have great flexibility, a genuine belief that there is good in every human being, and the ability to communicate with African-American youth and parents. The effective teachers are warm, outgoing, flexible, and supportive in their relations with their pupils so that the pupils will know and believe in their innate abilities.

Mentor teachers and inservice workshops can coach K-12 teachers to be complimentary but honest. More positive and caring attitudes toward African-American students and their parents can be encouraged at every opportunity. Every child, whether African-American or majority, comes to school with considerable potential and should be exposed to positive attitudes by all adults involved in the learning process.

When African-American students do not sense a positive and welcoming attitude in their teachers and administrators, they are likely to assume that the teachers do not like them. In turn, these students, particularly those in the early grade levels, may not live up to their academic potential in the classroom because they feel their teachers do not care for them. Many will simply refuse to work in the classroom. They will rebel by misbehaving and eventually will become turned off to academics. These children's perceptions of their teachers' attitudes may determine whether or not teachers will be successful in accomplishing class objectives.

In reflective activities in my inservice workshops, many new Anglo-American and new middle-class African-American teachers revealed that with the African-American students they were more reserved, had fewer positive interactions, and probably had lower expectations for the academic ability and behavior of these students. Their attitude was not deliberate, but unconscious, and, on reflection, they attributed it to media associations of African-American children with guns, crack cocaine, and violence. The teachers also attributed their own behaviors and attitudes to the facts that many of the children came from low-income backgrounds and many of the parents had drug and alcohol problems.

To facilitate reflection on attitudes, inservice programs should be initiated that observe and provide support for teachers in classrooms with significant numbers of African-American students. Also, if teachers do not have current information about the sociological and psychological aspects of African-American children from previous coursework, the inservice program might provide them with the opportunity to gain this knowledge. The sociological and psychological characteristics of the home, peers, language, and community of the students should be explored in this endeavor.

Without a doubt, one of the better ways to improve attitudes toward an entire group is to work with its members individually and learn that each one is a significant individual (Comer, 1987). Mentor teachers and inservice programs can encourage K-12 teachers to work with African-American community organizations and African-American churches to promote good attitudes.

Principals and the district personnel office should seek to prepare and recruit teachers with good interpersonal skills who will consistently display positive and caring attitudes toward African-American children inside and outside the classroom. Selection procedures could include interview questions to find out whether the teachers have the interpersonal skills and attitudes that are effective in interactions with African-American students. The Ethnic-Minority-Attitude Interview Questionnaire (EMAIQ) (see page 21) was field-tested with 22 urban principals to establish validity. The questions provide models of the kind that are appropriate to use as one of the criteria to screen teachers who will teach in schools with large numbers of urban African-American students.

EXPECTATIONS, RESPECT, AND AWARENESS

There are excellent initiatives that help K-12 teachers foster an environment marked by high expectations, respect, and cultural awareness of their multicultural students. First, it is important for teachers to understand the danger of the "self-fulfilling prophecy," and to understand how they can model behaviors denoting high but realistic expectations. According to

Good and Brophy (1991), the effects of self-fulfilling prophecies are powerful because they induce a significant change in student behavior.

The effects of a self-fulfilling prophecy can be seen when an originally erroneous expectation leads to behavior that causes the expectation to become true. What you expect, you get. Teacher expectations affect student learning.

Teachers who erroneously assume that African-American students cannot achieve will communicate their assumptions in numerous subtle ways. Their attitudes will undermine the opportunities of these students to achieve. African-American students will sense and then internalize their teachers' beliefs and reduce their efforts. Their achievement will be less than it would be if their teachers had begun with high expectations for their success. High expectations can lead to academic success for the African-American student.

When assigned to teach classes where many of the students were from poor and African-American homes, the teachers adjusted their instructional goals downward, used watered-down material to stress basic facts and skills, and replaced thought-provoking discussions with rote learning (Garton, 1984). To prevent educators from engaging in this type of debilitating self-fulfilling prophecy for their students, two reforms might be considered. The first reform is to revise the language that has traditionally been used to describe underachieving African-American students. The second reform is help teachers consistently model behaviors conveying high expectations.

The first reform is to avoid labeling African-American students—and all students—in any way. They should not be referred to as "high achievers," "low achievers," "at-risk populations," or "learning disabled," or by any other term that transforms them from a person into a category. Many African-American students of low socioeconomic status come from low-income homes where the environment contributes to low educational levels, poor motivation, and weak self-esteem, but they themselves are not born "high" and "low." Cultures are not "high" and "low." These stereotypes can be reversed by fostering an understanding of the home environment of the students and by focusing on the positive elements of different (not "lower") cultures.

Good and Brophy (1991) described many research-based examples of teachers unintentionally conveying low expectations to low-income and African-American students. Behaviors reflective of low expectations include the following:

(1) Waiting less time for minorities to answer questions (before giving the answers or calling on someone else);

(2) Providing fewer clues or follow-up questions when a child hesitates to answer;

(3) Praising a child less for successes and criticizing more for failures;

(4) Providing fewer challenging assignments;

(5) Asking minorities more lower-level questions (yes-no questions);

(6) Having fewer interactions with minority students;

(7) Giving fewer independent assignments;

(8) Being unfair in the application of classroom rules; and

(9) Calling on minority students fewer times to answer questions.

My own experiences confirm the research demonstrating that many teachers have lower expectations for African-Americans. The reasons are varied, but two major ones are the lack of inservice training on what to do for these students and a lack of support for teachers who have a substantial number of these students in their classes. Yet, when high achievement and high standards are expected of African-American students, they rise to the challenge.

When teachers unintentionally set low standards for African-American students' performance, they can expect these children to adopt these low standards. The mindset for low expectations has been profoundly ingrained in African-American students during the elementary- and middle-school years. By the time they reach high school, a significant number of these students really feel inferior.

These students are likely to go through life convinced that they cannot accomplish much. The teachers who expected less of them in the early school years have inadvertently set them up for failure. A mindset has been created that will affect the students throughout their adult lives.

All students are a little lazy, if they are allowed to be. Offered the chance to do less work, naturally they will accept. African-American students are street-smart enough to play the game. They will make up excuses for not completing challenging assignments. Teachers should not be fooled, however. All African-American students are capable of high achievement in school.

Effective teachers communicate high expectations to all students in an understandable manner beginning on the first day and continuing throughout the school year (Uchitelle, Bartz, & Hillman, 1989). They spell out the rules and procedures to students clearly and constructively in terms and examples they can understand. The teachers review the rules and procedures when necessary. They instruct the students how to be responsible for their own behavior in the classroom and other places on the school grounds. Effective educators use positive reinforcement to reward behavior. Systematic and ongoing communication of standards takes place with parents. These teachers communicate their belief that each African-American student has self-worth and can behave properly.

The Ethnic-Minority-Sensitive Expectations Checklist (EMSEC) was field-tested with 42 teachers from different grade levels to establish validity. It is designed to help teachers reflect about whether or not they are communicating high expectations to African-American students. Good and Brophy's (1991) research-based examples of teachers conveying low expectations to low-income and African-American students are reflected in the EMSEC's questions (see page 22).

Second, mentor teachers can help enhance K-12 teachers' respect for and understanding of the African-American children's culture. If the majority- or minority-culture teacher retains a strong belief in the superiority of one culture over any other culture, this attitude is subtly transmitted to the African-American student. This often causes the child to develop a poor self-concept. The Ethnic-Minority-Sensitive Respect Model (EMSRM) was field-tested with 27 teachers to establish validity. It provides questions to facilitate reflection in this area (see page 23).

Because many urban African-American students are street-smart, they can readily perceive teaching and classroom management behaviors symptomatic of the "better-than-you" attitude (Reglin, 1993a). Teachers can convince African-American students that they are not there to judge or categorize if they make efforts to combat and minimize the stereotypes and myths that prevail with regard to African-American children and detract from their ability to gain respect.

Educators should be encouraged to view these youth as culturally different or culturally diverse as opposed to culturally deprived or culturally disadvantaged. The latter two terms express an arrogant belief that these cultures function at a level inferior to the majority-group culture. It is not advisable to refer to underachieving African-American students as "at-risk" students. It is more appropriate to refer to them as students at risk or "students placed at risk." In speech and writing, teachers and administrators should avoid referring to the student as a "minority." Some people feel "minority" is denigrating and is associated with "being less than." The phrase "people of color" is no better and rings of the 1950s.

African-American children often live in two worlds, that of the dominant society and that of their own cultural group. They are sometimes confused about where they belong and where they want to be. Failure with African-American children is many times a failure to convey that they are held in dignity and respect, regardless of background.

In addition to conveying high expectations and developing respect for the culture of their students, it is important for teachers to realize the "power" they gain through awareness and knowledge. Their respect for different cultures can be strengthened through education that makes them aware of the African-American culture. Such knowledge can be used to establish a positive class atmosphere. Furthermore, teachers can make African-American students self-aware of some of their own behaviors that contribute to cultural conflict.

A perplexing situation for many African-American students is the choice between "acting Anglo-American"—adopting appropriate school attitudes and behaviors that enhance academic success but are perceived and interpreted by them as typical of Anglo-Americans—and acting African-American, which for them means adopting attitudes and behaviors that the African-American students consider appropriate for their group, but which are not necessarily supportive of academic success in school.

Wiley (1990) demonstrated one example of African-American male behavior that often arouses negative attitudes in the classroom. He stated that "Anglo-American people often look at the 'expressive lifestyle' (i.e., hundred-dollar sneakers, gold chains, gold rings on the fingers, and diamond ear rings) of African-American males as threatening, aggressive, and intimidating." This was due in large part to cultural misinterpretation of those behaviors. Teachers should be capable of recognizing this cultural clash and deal effectively deal with it.

Ogbu (1992) provides three strategies that will enhance awareness:

(1) Teachers can realize that many African-American students come to school with behaviors that are probably different from theirs and in opposition to those of the mainstream school.

(2) Special counseling programs and classroom strategies should be used to (a) help African-American students learn to separate attitudes and behaviors enhancing school success from those that lead to "acting Anglo-American" and (b) to help the students avoid interpreting conformity to the prevailing culture as a threat to their social identity and sense of security.

(3) School programs and classroom strategies are needed to increase students' willingness and success in adopting the strategy of accommodation without assimilation, or "playing the classroom game." The African-American students should be made to realize that they can participate in two cultural frames of reference for different purposes without undermining their loyalty to the African-American community. They must be taught "when in Rome, do as the Romans do," without becoming Romans.

K-12 teachers participating in group activities will augment their awareness of critical terms such as *culture, prejudice, stereotype,* and *discrimination.* Awareness and an understanding of these terms early in the teaching career will contribute substantially to eliminating future classroom cultural conflict. Four inservice directors field-tested the Ethnic-Minority-Sensitive Awareness Activities (EMSAA) with 93 teachers and found that they foster an awareness and an understanding of sensitive terms and statements (see page 24).

IMPLICATIONS

K-12 instruction and behaviors need to change comprehensively and fundamentally if they are to provide more productive teaching experiences for teachers and more successful learning experiences for minorities, especially urban African-American students. Many of the educational problems experienced by underachieving African-American students stem from a major function of school, that of controlling behavior. Traditional teacher-centered classroom tactics—lecturing, large-group instruction, reliance on a textbook and chalkboard, seat work assignments, recitation, and teacher-directed discussion—are designed to control behavior. Some African-American children's social behaviors and culturally derived expectations provide a good fit with the demands of this type of classroom. With many others, however, their behavioral characteristics are at odds with the classroom social norms and may lead to patterns of school failure (Taylor, 1991).

The chronic plight of African-American students in U.S. public schools has become critical. Because teachers play a central role in resolving it, their preparation must be a prime target of school restructuring. During workshops conducted in the public schools, I have often heard teachers say, "My professors in teacher education did not teach me what I needed to know to work effectively with African-American students in the classrooms."

These teachers expressed frustration in working with African-American students who are not motivated and who do not seem to care about themselves or their future. Their teacher-education programs did not prepare them to make successful connections between African-American families and students and themselves. The teachers did not understand the significant number of problems urban African-American children face in the home environment, which they are struggling to surmount.

Bennett (1990) focused on the miscues that occur between teachers and students because of misinterpretations and generalizations made about the background of culturally diverse students. These miscues caused much cultural conflict in classrooms. They are one major reason for the low achievement-test scores of African-American students.

In many of their educational experiences, African-Americans have suffered as a result of negative social, economic, and educational policies. Practices such as referral of these students in disproportionate numbers to special-education classes continue even today in many districts. Also, many African-American students have not been prepared by their parents to be comfortable working in a non-African-American environment. Many African-American students have concentrated solely on working on grades, rather than concentrating on social and affective strategies in interactions with teachers that tend to translate into higher grades.

America is rapidly changing. In most places, however, schools remain essentially the same as they have been since the Civil War. If schools are to serve urban African-American students, they will have to make a quantum leap forward. This will require a radical departure from the superficial alteration that was and is the norm. It will require that schools revolutionize their basic purpose of instruction. This revolution must be based on the strategies in this text. The time is more than now; it is past due.

This chapter should guide the K-12 teacher to ask further questions or request technical assistance to deliver appropriate instruction and to teach and model appropriate behaviors before a discipline referral is written on an African-American student. Strategies in the chapter will cause schools to be places where teachers and African-American students embrace the contributions of each other. Schools will be seen as places where people will want to go and stay, and where lifelong learning will be practiced.

ETHNIC-MINORITY-ATTITUDE INTERVIEW QUESTIONNAIRE (EMAIQ)

Rationale: The EMAIQ is a model of the kinds of questions which can be asked when interviewing teachers to work in schools with large numbers of African-American students. The questions are designed for both majority-culture and minority-culture teachers to ascertain their interpersonal skills and attitudes, which are critical when teaching African-American youth.

Directions: The principal or district personnel office representative asks the questions of the candidate and writes a brief summary of the responses. The responses are combined with other assessment tools to determine whether or not to hire the candidate.

1. Briefly discuss any volunteer community work you have done involving interactions with African-Americans and your response to these interactions.

   _____

   _____

2. How would you describe your personality? Do you think of yourself as introverted or extroverted, shy or outgoing? What are some reasons for your self-characterization?

   _____

   _____

3. To what extent are you willing to visit the homes of African-American students to meet with the parents or family members? How do you think you'd feel as you prepared for such a meeting?

   _____

   _____

4. How do you feel about attending community events with mostly African-American adult members after school hours?

   _____

   _____

5. How comfortable do you feel about visiting and phoning African-American sororities, fraternities, churches, and other organizations that are potential sources of African-American mentors, tutors, and guest speakers? How would you go about inviting these individuals into your class to help with your students?

   _____

   _____

ETHNIC-MINORITY-SENSITIVE EXPECTATIONS CHECKLIST (EMSEC)

Rationale: Attitudes of teachers can unintentionally communicate low expectations to African-American students that lead to subpar motivation and achievement.

Directions: A mentor teacher should review all items on the checklist with the teacher to ensure understanding and then observe the teacher teach a lesson to evaluate his or her behaviors by circling **yes, somewhat,** or **no** on the EMSEC. **Somewhat**s and **no**s should be discussed and the teacher should be encouraged to write a plan to remedy these items before a subsequent observation.

1. Proper use of wait-time. After calling on African-American students, did the educator wait three to five seconds to give them sufficient time to respond?

a = Yes   b = Somewhat   c = No

2. Helping with incorrect or incomplete answers. When African-American students gave incorrect or incomplete answers to questions, did the teacher probe further with a series of questions to help the students locate the correct answer?

a = Yes   b = Somewhat   c = No

3. Giving specific praise. Did the educator give specific praise designed to reinforce the academic performance of the African-American students?

a = Yes   b = Somewhat   c = No

4. Challenging assignments. Does the teacher make sure that African-American students get challenging assignments? (Assignments that are too easy suggest a lack of confidence in the students' abilities.)

a = Yes   b = Somewhat   c = No

5. Asking open-ended, thought-provoking questions instead of "yes-no" questions. Does the teacher ask the students open-ended, thought-provoking questions requiring them to apply, evaluate, analyze, or synthesize information?

a = Yes   b = Somewhat   c = No

6. Interactions on a one-to-one basis and/or while in groups. Does the teacher interact equally with African-American students and majority-culture students in the classroom on a one-to-one basis and/or while students are working in small groups?

a = Yes   b = Somewhat   c = No

7. Developing independence, not dependence. Does the teacher give African-American students every opportunity to complete a new activity by themselves? (The teacher accomplishes this by demonstrating the task again or rephrasing the instructions instead of doing the task for the students.)

a = Yes   b = Somewhat   c = No

8. Applying rules consistently and fairly. Does the teacher punish African-American students for behaviors that are acceptable in the other students? (All students should know the rules and be held accountable for the rules.)

a = Yes   b = Somewhat   c = No

9. Calling on students to answer questions. Does the teacher call on African-American students less often than majority-culture students for answers?

a = Yes   b = Somewhat   c = No

ETHNIC-MINORITY-SENSITIVE RESPECT MODEL (EMSRM)

Rationale: If a "better-than-you attitude" is subtly transmitted, the teacher will be unable to establish a warm and supportive classroom climate for urban African-American students. To promote respect for these students, K-12 educators guided into reflecting on questions such as those that follow will be helped to develop respect for their students (Gay, 1988).

Directions: During a workshop, the facilitator or mentor teacher should either project as an overhead (see page 28) or give copies of the following questions to teachers to reflect on and discuss in groups. A recorder should be designated in each group to summarize the responses to each question in writing. A spokesperson from each group can present the group's responses for each question. This activity requires about 30 minutes.

HOW MUCH DO I RESPECT MY STUDENTS' BACKGROUNDS?

(1)   Am I aware of the important cultural factors in my African-American students' environment?

(2)   Do I accept African-American students' values?

(3)   Am I trying to make African-American students behave according to the cultural behaviors that I acquired from my environment?

(4)   Are my performance expectations for African-American learners similar to those for mainstream students?

(5)   Do I model behaviors clearly conveying a sense of respect for African-Americans as individuals with legitimate cultures?

ETHNIC-MINORITY-SENSITIVE AWARENESS ACTIVITIES (EMSAA)
(A WORKSHOP PLAN)

A group facilitator or inservice leader should direct these activities in workshops.

Objectives:

(1) To create an awareness of the definition/description of ethnic-minority-sensitive instruction and behaviors.

(2) To expand teachers' awareness of experiences which affect our understandings of ourselves and others.

(3) To facilitate teachers' awareness of the definitions of *prejudice, stereotype,* and *discrimination.*

---

1. ACTIVITY FOR OBJECTIVE NUMBER ONE—BRAINSTORMING IN GROUPS

Directions: Small groups should reflect on and discuss the following question:

"What are ethnic-minority-sensitive instruction and behaviors?"

A recorder for each group should write the group's responses on paper. A spokesperson then presents each group's responses to the large group. After all presentations are completed, Banks' adapted comprehensive description is displayed on an overhead (see page 29), or copies of the description (below) are circulated.

The entire group then discusses how well the small groups' responses fit with Banks' comprehensive definition.

INSTRUCTION AND BEHAVIORS SENSITIVE TO ETHNIC MINORITIES

Adapted from J. A. Banks. 1993. Multicultural education: Development, dimensions, and challenges. *Phi Delta Kappan,* 75(1), 22–28.

(1) **Content integration:** planning and implementing of lessons using examples, data, and information from the African-American culture to illustrate the key concepts and principles in a subject area.

(2) **Knowledge construction:** a process in which students are helped to understand how knowledge is created and how it is influenced by factors of ethnicity and social class.

(3) **Prejudice reduction:** the use of strategies and experiences to help students develop more positive racial and ethnic attitudes.

(4) **Equity pedagogy:** the use of techniques and teaching methods that facilitate the academic achievement of African-Americans, including cooperative learning (Shade, 1989).

(5) **Empowering school culture and social culture:** such measures as the adoption of assessment techniques that are fair to all groups, the abolition of tracking, and the creation of a belief among staff members that all students can learn.

2. ACTIVITY FOR OBJECTIVE NUMBER TWO—BECOMING AWARE OF DIVERSITY

Directions: The six categories of information (below) are displayed on an overhead (see page 30) or written on a flip chart. Each participant introduces himself or herself to the group by standing up and giving the information about him- or herself in order of the categories listed.

As the information is given, the facilitator completes a frequency table on items two through six by tallying the number of men and women, numbers in each income range, etc. The frequency table is displayed on the board and the group discusses

- what it reveals about the diversity of the groups in the room

- how different groups and individuals have different strengths

- how groups, individuals, and classes can capitalize on the strengths inherent in diversity.

Each person in the group could also be encouraged to describe his or her first experience of becoming aware of people being culturally different than him- or herself.

INFORMATION CATEGORIES

1) Name

2) Gender

3) Family income level (low, middle, or high)

4) Kind of neighborhood you grew up in (rural, suburban, or urban)

5) How you define yourself culturally

6) How you define yourself religiously

3. ACTIVITY FOR OBJECTIVE NUMBER THREE —DEFINITIONS

Directions: The following words ("Three Terms") should be displayed on an overhead (see page 31) with the definitions covered up, or written on the board or flip chart without definitions. In small groups, participants should brainstorm definitions for each.

After 30 minutes, the definitions and examples are uncovered on the overhead. Definitions can be written on the board or flip chart and the examples given orally.

The groups should then compare and contrast the definitions and examples given with those they have generated in their groups.

Each participant should then think of a specific experience in which he or she was the victim of prejudice, stereotyping, or discrimination. Each should write a one- to two-page summary of what occurred and what feelings were engendered. They then read their accounts to other members of their groups. Together the groups discuss these experiences by asking each other

• What are some of the feelings you experienced when this incident happened?

• Do you think your feelings are similar to those of others in the class? Why or why not?

• Why do people show prejudice, discriminate against others, or stereotype others? How can we or they change?

THREE TERMS

Prejudice   An unfavorable opinion about a person or group of people formed without knowledge.

John says, "I hate African-Americans!"

John has never met African-Americans. He is prejudiced against African-Americans.

Stereotype   A general viewpoint about a group of people not based on fact.

Stereotype: Elderly African-American people are always sick and always need relatives to care for them.

Fact: Many elderly African-American people are healthy and independent. Other elderly African-American persons have illnesses and need assistance.

Discrimination   Actions which deny people or particular groups resources based on race, sex, class, age, or physical ability, thus guaranteeing unequal life outcomes.

Discrimination, then, sets up unequal situations, often blaming the victim: "If I did it, so can you," or "You could make it if you'd only try," or "Everyone has an equal opportunity."

4.   CULMINATING ACTIVITY—LARGE-GROUP DISCUSSION

Directions: With the participants assembled in the large group, the facilitator has them synthesize the knowledge they have gained in activities 1, 2, and 3. Each participant is asked to contribute at least five important strategies that would significantly improve a lesson, classroom management procedure, cultural awareness, classroom climate, classroom discipline procedure, or teaching behavior in a setting with African-American students.

Participants should be encouraged to lead into each statement about a strategy or behavior with one of the following sentence openers. These can also be posted or displayed on an overhead (see page 32):

WHAT I HAVE LEARNED

I learned that I...

I realized that I...

I noticed that I...

I was pleased that I...

I was aware that I...

HOW MUCH DO I RESPECT MY STUDENTS' BACKGROUNDS?

(1) Am I aware of the important cultural factors in my African-American students' environment?

(2) Do I accept African-American students' values?

(3) Am I trying to make African-American students behave according to the cultural behaviors that I acquired from my environment?

(4) Are my performance expectations for African-American learners similar to those for mainstream students?

(5) Do I model behaviors clearly conveying a sense of respect for African-Americans as individuals with legitimate cultures?

INSTRUCTION AND BEHAVIORS SENSITIVE TO ETHNIC MINORITIES

Adapted from J. A. Banks. 1993. Multicultural education: Development, dimensions, and challenges. *Phi Delta Kappan,* 75(1), 22-28:

(1) **Content integration:** planning and implementing of lessons using examples, data, and information from the African-American culture to illustrate the key concepts and principles in a subject area.

(2) **Knowledge construction:** a process in which students are helped to understand how knowledge is created and how it is influenced by factors of ethnicity and social class.

(3) **Prejudice reduction:** the use of strategies and experiences to help students develop more positive racial and ethnic attitudes.

(4) **Equity pedagogy:** the use of techniques and teaching methods that facilitate the academic achievement of African-Americans, including cooperative learning (Shade, 1989).

(5) **Empowering school culture and social culture:** such measures as the adoption of assessment techniques that are fair to all groups, the abolition of tracking, and the creation of a belief among staff members that all students can learn.

INFORMATION CATEGORIES

(1) Name

(2) Gender

(3) Family income level (low, middle, or high)

(4) Kind of neighborhood you grew up in (rural, suburban, or urban)

(5) How you define yourself culturally

(6) How you define yourself religiously

THREE TERMS

Prejudice   An unfavorable opinion about a person or group of people formed without knowledge.

John says, "I hate African-Americans!"
John has never met African-Americans. He is prejudiced against African-Americans.

Stereotype   A general viewpoint about a group of people not based on fact.

Stereotype: Elderly African-American people are always sick and always need relatives to care for them.

Fact: Many elderly African-American people are healthy and independent. Other elderly African-American persons have illnesses and need assistance.

Discrimination   Actions which deny people or particular groups resources based on race, sex, class, age, or physical ability, thus guaranteeing unequal life outcomes.

Discrimination, then, sets up unequal situations, often blaming the victim: "If I did it, so can you," or "You could make it if you'd only try," or "Everyone has an equal opportunity."

WHAT I HAVE LEARNED

I learned that I...

I realized that I...

I noticed that I...

I was pleased that I...

I was aware that I...

ACTIVITIES FOR READERS OF CHAPTER ONE

1. There are behaviors of teachers that unintentionally communicate low expectations to African-American students. Plan and teach a lesson to a class with at least 30 percent African-American students. Request that a mentor teacher observe your lesson using an instrument modeled on the Ethnic-Minority-Sensitive Expectations Checklist (EMSEC, see page 22). Ask the mentor teacher to evaluate your teaching behaviors by circling "yes," "somewhat," or "no" on the checklist. Discuss all "some-whats" and "nos" in a conference with the mentor teacher and seek advice on improving these. If "yes" was checked fewer than eight times, write a plan with the help of the mentor teacher to remedy all "somewhats" and "nos." Then request another observation. Write a one- or two-page paper reflecting on the differences in the two observed teaching experiences. In your paper, discuss the changes you made and any changes in the African-American students' behavior.

2. At an inservice training session or in small (four-member) informal discussion groups with colleagues, reflect on and discuss questions such as those on the Ethnic-Minority-Sensitive Respect Model (EMSRM) (Gay, 1988), page 23, to pro-mote respect for urban African-American students in the classroom.

   Designate a recorder in each group to summarize the responses to each question in writing. Allow 30 minutes for the group work. A spokesperson from each group can then present the group's responses to each question. After all groups have presented their responses, the inservice coordinator or mentor teacher should ask three questions to all groups.

   • Did the members of any group respond similarly to a question?

   • Did any group member learn something new about his or her behavior as a result of this reflective process?

   • How can the responses from the group lead to promoting respect for African-American students in the classroom?

Suggested Readings for Chapter One

Banks, J.A. (1993). Multicultural education: Development, dimensions, and challenges. *Phi Delta Kappan,* 75(1), 22-28.

Ogbu, J. (1990). Minority education in comparative perspective. *Journal of Negro Education,* 59(1), 46-49.

Ogbu, J.U. (1992). Understanding cultural differences and school learning. *Educational Libraries,* 16(3), 7-11.

Reglin, G.L. (1993). *Motivating low-achieving students: A special focus on unmotivated and under-achieving African-American students.* Springfield, IL.: Charles C. Thomas, Publisher.

Valverde, L.A. (1993). Philosophy of student acculturation. *Education and Urban Society,* 25(3), 246-253.

New and Adapted Teaching Strategies for Multicultural Students

Chapter Two Objectives

After reading this chapter, readers should be able to:

Describe the relationship between three instructional planning components: Daily Lesson Plan Outline, Ethnic-Minority-Sensitive Checklist, and Reflections on Strengths and Weaknesses.

State three techniques used to discover the interests of African-American students.

Describe the strengths of cooperative learning.

Describe several strategies effective in molding a warm and supportive climate for African-American students.

Identify two climate enhancers.

Explain why peer mediation is helpful to African-American students.

OVERVIEW OF TEACHING REFORMS

Teaching strategies and techniques can be adopted or adapted to be more supportive of the needs of African-American students. The teaching techniques described in detail in this chapter include the following:

- planning lessons inclusive of African-American culture
- planning lessons that capitalize on African-American students' interests
- planning cooperative-learning (CL) activities
- teaching social skills
- understanding the effect of school and class climate
- modeling caring
- modeling attitudes and behaviors that reduce a chilly school climate
- assessing the school and classroom climate
- implementing initiatives to enhance a more positive climate
- assessing the media for stereotyping
- resolving conflicts arising from ethnic differences
- organizing a portfolio of interactions with African-Americans

PLANNING LESSONS INCLUSIVE OF AFRICAN-AMERICAN CULTURE

The Ethnic-Minority-Sensitive Lesson Plan (EMSLP) will help teachers plan lessons sensitive to the African-American culture. The EMSLP is a model for a three-component framework used to plan lessons for classrooms that include African-American students. The three components should be keyed into a word processor to set up computerized templates so that the teacher will be able to create or modify lesson plans as needed.

Component I (Daily Lesson Plan Outline, see page 48) of the EMSLP provides a blueprint for developing the lesson plan. Each item in Component I must be addressed in writing for all lessons. Component II (Ethnic-Minority-Sensitive Checklist, page 49) constitutes a checklist for review of the lesson plan to assess its ethnic sensitivity. As many colleagues as possible should be enlisted to review the lesson plan. Component III (Reflections on Strengths and Weaknesses, page 50), to be completed after the teacher has taught the lesson, provides a format for evaluating the strengths and weaknesses of the lesson.

The mentor teacher must review Components I and II at least three days before the classroom teacher presents the lesson. The mentor teacher should discuss Component III with the teacher after the lesson has been taught. This component is a quality-control check for sensitivity to an ethnic minority that must be undertaken upon completion of Components I and II by the classroom teacher. Components I and II ideally should be reviewed by small groups of urban African-American teachers who can help determine if cultural bias exists.

Another quality-control check option is to ask university professors in the teacher-education program to review Components I and II. After the quality-control checks, the classroom teacher needs to examine why he or she made inappropriate choices and then must develop strategies for eliminating such misjudgments in the future. Teachers should continue to plan lessons using the eight questions in Component I of the EMSLP.

PLANNING LESSONS THAT CAPITALIZE ON AFRICAN-AMERICAN STUDENTS' INTERESTS

Many unmotivated and underachieving African-American students do not understand activities in lesson plans that make no connection to their interests and experiences. Each lesson plan should reflect as much about the interests and experiences of the African-American students as possible. This will somewhat narrow the gap between student and teacher. There are many ways teachers can learn about the varied interests and experiences of their African-American students, including inventories, class discussions, and teacher-student discussions. The teacher should find out about the heroes, favorite sports, and hobbies of their African-American students by making a point to talk to them after class in the halls and at after-school events (ball games, dances, etc.).

In large classes, staff members can spend the first five or ten minutes of class every day having the students share what has happened in their lives since the day before. Sometimes this session may be longer as personal problems arise—but it will be important to the students.

Additional techniques for learning about students include having students write a classified advertisement that could be used to sell themselves, designating a student-of-the-week, and listening while students talk in groups. Teachers will find that nearly all the students have the same interests: sports, music, and being with friends. The major differences will probably be cultural, such as the type of music or the specific sport they like. For instance, while they all may enjoy loud music, different groups may prefer different styles, ranging from country to rap.

The four Ethnic-Minority Classroom Interest Inventories (EMCIIs), contained among the reproducible models at the end of this chapter, have been useful for uncovering African-American students' interests and experiences in order to integrate them into the lesson plan (see pages 51-54). The EMCIIs are valuable not only for planning lessons but also for planning cooperative groups. They are good to use when looking for positive reinforcement that is effective for classes with African-American students. They will provide teachers with information that will make lessons relevant and interesting for classrooms.

To administer the Inventories, teachers should select the EMCII that they feel will collect the best data and administer it during the first two weeks of class to create a profile of interests and experiences for their classes. This profile can be used when planning all lessons. Interest Inventory Number Four (see page 54) is for non-readers in grades 1, 2, and 3. It is to be administered by reading the questions to the students on a one-to-one basis with the teacher or other adult recording the responses.

PLANNING COOPERATIVE-LEARNING (CL) LESSONS

Mentoring programs that help teachers learn cooperative-learning strategies are invaluable for teachers. Cooperative learning (CL) is defined as students working together in groups (often followed by a teacher-presented lesson), with group goals and individual accountability. The groups are organized to include both high- and low-achieving students, Anglo-Americans and African-Americans, and males and females. They work together to be rewarded as a team, as well as individually, for their achievement and improvement (Tyrrell, 1990). This technique involves students' receiving rewards or recognition for their individual as well as their group performance.

Cooperative learning helps students from different backgrounds become friends. It is also helpful in learning academic content, developing cognitive skills, developing social skills, and enhancing character education. There is evidence that CL has a positive effect on classroom climate, self-esteem among students, internal locus of control, role-taking abilities, attendance, and the attitude toward learning among African-American students (Johnson, Johnson, & Holubec, 1988).

CL is a viable alternative to ability grouping and tracking. It is estimated that only 10 percent of all teachers are using cooperative learning (Wilson, 1992), but cooperative learning is spreading fast and becoming more prevalent, as evidenced by the tremendous demand for training among educators.

CL strategies are currently being used in a number of classrooms across the country to build on African-American students' strengths. It changes power relationships in the classroom and shifts the responsibility for learning from the teacher to the student (Slavin, 1983). In their groups, stronger students find working with and helping weaker ones intellectually stimulating and enriching. Stronger students' academic achievement continues to increase as they engage in the process of explaining the material to their teammates. Sometimes students are better educators because they can simplify or bring content down to a level of understanding for other students.

Stronger students also improve because of the need to use higher-level thinking skills to teach others. The weaker students find that their classroom exertion is important. They discover that whatever they contribute can help the team effort. CL works with all students. The Ethnic-Minority-Sensitive Cooperative-Learning Activities (EMSCLA) will help teachers work effectively with African-American students (see page 55). The EMSCLA should be used with the Ethnic-Minority-Sensitive Cooperative Checklist (EMSCC, see pages 56-57).

TEACHING SOCIAL SKILLS

Teaching social skills in the classroom is important. Once mastered, such skills will reduce conflict in the classrooms and promote an atmosphere of trust and understanding. Students don't learn well without certain social skills (Brigman, 1993).

Many African-Americans come into the classroom lacking social skills. Children who lack these skills tend to be unsuccessful in school and cause the most discipline problems. There is a strong positive relationship between social skills and school success. By teaching children the skills they need for social and academic success, teachers will increase student achievement and decrease misbehavior.

An excellent research base supports findings that certain social skills and attitudes (a) are critically important to school success; (b) can be taught most effectively in the regular classroom by the classroom teacher; and (c) result in children learning more effectively and working more cooperatively when the skills are taught directly and systematically (Brigman, 1993). Examples of important social skills include listening and attending, encouragement, social-problem solving, conflict management, and group discussion.

Teachers can promote the learning of social skills by taking the following steps (see also page 58):

STEPS FOR TEACHING SOCIAL SKILLS

1. The desired social skills should be explicit and clearly defined with concrete positive and negative examples.

2. Training and practice in the skills should be built into, complement, and support the regular curriculum. Teachers should explain what the students are to do, demonstrate the skills, and have the students practice them with coaching and feedback from the teacher.

3. Opportunities should be provided for self-directed and guided application and evaluation (e.g., story telling/listening in pairs, cooperative learning, peer tutoring, and service learning).

4. Students need opportunities for making choices and decisions related to the classroom. They can actively participate in establishing class rules, weekly class meetings, and encouragement councils.

There are many programs and resources available to help student teachers promote self-discipline by teaching social skills and learning skills. Several are listed at the end of this chapter.

UNDERSTANDING THE EFFECT OF SCHOOL AND CLASS CLIMATE

According to R. Edmonds (1979), a leader of Effective Schools research, an effective school is characterized by a school climate that brings an equal percentage of its highest and lowest social classes to minimum mastery and promotes high expectations for all students. Even though this Effective Schools research was shared with educators many years ago, a disproportionate number of African-American students still lag behind Anglo-American students in achievement measures, largely because of the unchanged climate in the public schools. The school climate continues to reflect middle-class Anglo-American culture and values.

Several important factors perpetuate a climate oriented toward the middle-class and simultaneously fuel the subpar academic motivation and achievement of many African-American students. In many schools high expectations are assumed for the majority Anglo-American students while the expectations for both academics and behaviors of many African-American students remain low.

Often, the climate of a school reflects middle-class Anglo-American culture. Frequently, nearly all teachers are Anglo-American middle-class females. Few teachers receive training to prepare them for the encounter with the cultural diversity that is thrust upon them when African-American students come into the classroom. The results can be limited patience, discipline referrals, attempts to track the students into special-education programs, and teaching at a distance.

Because of inadequate preservice training, some teachers may have difficulty teaching to the social and psychological needs of these students. Moreover, many principals have not understood the importance of taking measures to improve the climate of expectations, cultural acceptance, and recognizing student needs.

Principals are of utmost significance in shaping and controlling the school climate by putting their fingerprints on the schools. Effective climates created for teachers by principals will encourage and help teachers to build equally positive climates for African-American students. Crucial to this effort is a conviction that all students can and do want to learn. Administrators, like their teachers, should convey their certainty that, while many African-American families may not have the home space and furniture to provide study areas, they will indeed make sacrifices to help their offspring gain an education.

The school climate must reflect the African-American students' culture. African-American students feel a sense of discomfort because the culture of the school is vastly different from the culture of their community. There are several specific strategies that teachers can use to instill respect for the African-American culture in the school. Students engaging in overt racial prejudice should be disciplined. Events promoting good racial harmony must be held in the school at every opportunity.

I suggest that teachers have extensive personal contacts with African-American students in the school. These contacts can take place in the halls and at sporting events involving substantial numbers of African-American students. Student contact is a top priority in shaping a good climate.

According to Cummins (1986), African-American students do not fail when they are positively oriented toward both their own and the dominant culture, when they do not perceive themselves as inferior to the dominant group, and when they are not alienated from their own cultural values. Teachers can shape the content and process of instruction around the experiences of their students and address cultural relevance in all aspects of student learning. Basic skills and higher-order thinking skills need not be neglected in these practices. Rather, curriculum and instruction that are meaningful to students enhance knowledge acquisition and promote cultural diversity.

There is an affective dimension of all school climates, which is shaped by working on interpersonal skills. In fact, an increasing body of literature emphasizes the importance of affective states among African-American students and the need for intervention strategies to address these as primary goals. Effective schools are beginning to realize that academic achievement is only one dimension in the success profile of a school. The evidence shows an increasing awareness that interpersonal skills depend on affective states. These are important concerns that need to be given much greater attention (Prawat, 1985).

African-American students, like mainstream students, have psycho-social needs which teachers need to be prepared to address. Emmer, Evertson, & Anderson (1980) reported that students gave higher ratings to teachers who were warmer, more caring, and more supportive. These teachers placed high priority on the affective climate of their classrooms.

There is strong evidence that psychological well-being among students is significantly and positively related to academic achievement (Evertson, Anderson, & Brophy, 1980). There are several specific strategies that all educators should employ in this area, such as turning attention and skill to developing human consideration instead of just emphasizing the content skills.

The best way to nurture human relationships and elevate the psychological element is for all educators to model the appropriate behaviors and then encourage all students to behave in the same way. They can make time to visit with African-American students throughout the school day, during lunch, before school, and after school. No type of insensitivity, such as calling a kid a failure, should be tolerated. Teachers should be guided into internalizing the role of guardian—and even parent—of these children to the extent that they become advocates for "their" children's success. Other improvements such as test scores and achievement gains may lag behind until the climate becomes strong and stable enough to generate, encourage, and support further progress (Comer, 1987).

MODELING CARING

Teachers can establish and maintain positive and nurturing classroom climates. Modeling the extension of a helping hand is a powerful tool in promoting a warm and supportive climate. When African-American students see teachers consistently helping other African-American students succeed in school, a positive climate is fostered. Such support can be accomplished by devoting a significant amount of time to counseling students and assisting them in making the rigorous adjustment to academic life.

It can happen in a school that an African-American student may not be in a particular teacher's class, but this teacher may overhear a colleague in the lounge discussing difficulties he or she is having with the student. In this case, the first teacher may be able to contact the student and offer some advice. The fact that someone has gone above and beyond the call of duty to assist the child will spread to other culturally diverse students in the school. The action will pay tremendous dividends in the classroom because African-American students will perceive that a teacher is caring and supportive. They will become more receptive to the teaching, participate more in class discussions, and ask more questions. There will be no fear of embarrassment for giving a wrong answer.

A "teacher of the year" shared an experience with me concerning her African-American students. The teacher frequently saw an African-American girl, Tanya, going to and from her classes looking depressed. She made a point of asking some of Tanya's teachers in the teachers' lounge about the girl's grades. She discovered that Tanya was stressed out because she was in jeopardy of failing her math and history classes.

The teacher of the year convinced Tanya to meet with the principal and the teachers of these two classes about her concerns. All agreed that there were communication problems. Together they discovered that Tanya prepared poorly for tests and had trouble making good grades on homework because her language barrier made it difficult for her to understand the directions provided in class. This situation was resolved when the teachers assigned a high-achieving majority-culture student to check with Tanya to see if she had any questions about her assignments at the end of the day. The majority-culture student functioned effectively as a class buddy.

The teacher of the year made it a point to meet with Tanya frequently to see if there was anything she could do to clarify directions and instructions presented in class. Tanya's grades improved. She began to feel good about school. She even felt good about the math and history classes. Tanya informed other African-American students, some of whom were in the teacher of the year's class, how helpful this educator had been in resolving her crisis.

All this information sharing contributed to the teacher of the year's having a much better multicultural classroom environment. There were few discipline problems from the African-American students. Another positive aspect of this matter was that Tanya learned to seek counseling from the other teachers frequently whenever a problem arose during the lesson. She gained more confidence in both subject areas and was able to experience many successes.

MODELING ATTITUDES AND BEHAVIORS THAT REDUCE A CHILLY CLIMATE

African-American students must perceive the classroom climate as being free of public embarrassment and criticism. Teachers should be aware that one negative remark made to an African-American student may quickly damage this type of atmosphere. For example, a teacher who was returning papers once remarked, "I expected Keito to have written a better, well-rounded essay with fewer deficiencies than were present." Keito is an African-American student. The comment upset the African-American students. If the remark had been counterbalanced quickly with positive statements, or if the teacher had apologized to Keito in front of the class or in private, these corrective measures could have reduced or eliminated the chilly climate.

African-American students and majority-culture students may perceive the class climate differently because these students have different needs. Feelings of trust, honesty, discipline, respect, and care must be present at all times for all students. Teachers can establish and maintain a climate that will promote heightened feelings of success, self-esteem, self-worth, and self-confidence.

Any deviation from a positive and accepting climate in a classroom can cause African-American students to have a negative change in attitude. In addition to negative remarks in class contributing to a chilly climate, a teacher losing patience with African-American students in front of the class can change the climate and affect all African-Americans in the class. It is important to be patient with all students and to model appropriate behaviors in the classrooms.

The Ethnic-Minority Climate-Building Initiatives (EMCBI) will assist in molding a warm and supportive classroom and school climate (see page 59). Teachers should model these behaviors or extend a helping hand by following the nine suggestions of the initiative in their interactions with African-American students.

Assessing the Climate

Educators should not assume that all African-American students perceive the classroom climate as being warm and supportive. Their perception of the climate can be assessed by asking questions, observing students for signs of dissatisfaction, and administering classroom-climate surveys to all students four times a year. These surveys should be brief, uncomplicated (such as a Likert scale), and capable of being quantified (data that can be tabulated). When findings indicate a chilly climate, educators should immediately take corrective measures, such as identifying the unhappy students and meeting them in private to find out the reasons for their perceptions of a chilly climate.

There are times when African-American students may misinterpret a teacher's behavior or comments. They may become upset with the teacher, but feel afraid to address this concern in the presence of any adult. The three Classroom-Climate Inventories (CCIs, pages 60-62) will help in analyzing this type of climate.

Using Climate Enhancers

Two types of climate enhancers have been shown to be effective. The first involves a concerted effort to make positive statements about students frequently. The second is based on the use of quotations chosen to generate discussion and followed by rationales. Both are important in establishing and maintaining a warm and supportive climate, which is essential to the achievement of African-American students.

Teachers need to be coached to make positive statements about their African-American students when they are in the classroom. They should also make statements of this sort in the presence of their colleagues in such places as the teachers' lounge, the cafeteria, and at faculty meetings. The statements are more effective with elementary- and middle-school students than with high-school students. Care should be taken not to over-praise high-school students. Over-praising may cause students to discount future attempts at praise as being insincere and having little meaning for them. Examples of positive, climate-enhancing statements are listed on the reproducible model, "Climate-Enhancing Statements" (see page 63).

Taking a few minutes at the beginning of class to discuss an inspirational or thought-provoking quotation—one that has relevance to the students' lives and is similar to those listed in the reproducible "Quotations and Rationales" (see page 64) can enhance the classroom climate and make students more receptive to the lesson. Such quotations can be displayed on the chalkboard or an overhead to generate discussion.

ASSESSING THE MEDIA FOR STEREOTYPING

A stereotype is an oversimplified generalization about a particular group, race, or sex that generally carries a derogatory implication. Stereotypes distort and falsify our perceptions of members of other groups, oversimplify complex relationships, or present only one side of a multifaceted reality. Teachers can study television programs, movies, music videos, music lyrics, and other entertainment popular with the age group they are preparing to teach to examine the depiction of cultural bias, stereotypical behaviors, and negative treatment (Rubalcava, 1991). They could then discuss ways they might help students realize any negative societal consequences of cultural misrepresentation by the media (Ravitch, 1991).

When studying the media, teachers can be encouraged to point out to students that the media have created a negative image of African-American children through stereotypes, omissions, and distortions. For example, for many years an African-American actor or actress was allowed to portray only such stereotypic roles as servant or laborer. The news media continue to support biased reporting.

Anglo-Americans involved in criminal activities seldom are identified by ethnicity—only name, age, and sex. Their pictures are seldom published in the newspaper, and rarely on the front page. When African-Americans commit crimes, however, their race is usually mentioned and their photos often printed. This biased reporting sends erroneous messages to the world that African-Americans are responsible for most of the criminal activity. History books are also filled with omissions, distortions, and stereotyping.

Many African-American children lack positive role models to identify with, either in the home, on the television screen, on the movie screen, or in the newspaper. Consequently, they learn to perceive themselves and their cultural group as inferior to the majority culture. Economically and politically, many view themselves as powerless. Vocationally, they may be conditioned to limit themselves to such roles as domestic worker, laundry man, migrant farm worker, or criminal. Socially, African-American youngsters may perceive themselves as existing on the margins of society.

Teachers may have to rectify many of the negative self-concepts derived from years of media exposure to stereotypes, omissions, and distortions. Educators should help all school children to recognize and understand stereotypes.

When students can identify an ethnic stereotype in a story or film—even if they cannot yet supply the correct information or perspective—they will be alerted to the fact that the whole truth is not being told and that a quest must be undertaken to find out what the whole truth is. Students will be less influenced by stereotypes the more they recognize them for what they are.

RESOLVING CONFLICTS FROM ETHNIC DIFFERENCES

Teachers can study conflict resolution using such texts as Fisher and Ury's *Getting to Yes.* They can then study actual conflicts in a school setting or tapes of actual conflicts to determine whether the conflicts are related to or exacerbated by ethnic differences. Then they can apply strategies for conflict resolution. If such conflicts are determined to be real, the teacher could develop and deliver instruction to the students applying these strategies. Teachers might actually have the students engage in a performance task dealing with identifying and resolving conflicts.

Peer mediation is a positive approach to dealing with inappropriate behaviors, especially aggression and conflicts between students. Peer mediation offers students a way to solve problems without violence (Wampler, 1993) and frees teachers to teach. Students are taught to use active-listening skills and communication techniques to help disputing students come to agreement. The four-step process includes setting the ground rules, storytelling, problem solving, and coming to agreement. The "brightest" students in class should not necessarily be first choices as mediators. Students who get along well with others may be better choices. Mediators don't try to conclude who's right or wrong. Mediation is one of the choices to consider from the pool of conflict-resolution options, which also includes negotiation and creative problem solving.

The mediation process is helpful to African-American students because it empowers them to solve their own conflicts rather than expect someone else to do it for them. If students are working through relationship problems which occur in school, mediation frees the staff to teach and creates a more positive environment within the school. This positive aspect frequently carries over into the community, particularly when the community supports the school program by providing other opportunities to use mediation. These opportunities may include parent-child mediations, which can be referred by the school, the court, or the parties involved.

Peer mediation in a school offers African-American students the means to work through problems independently. It's an opportunity to experience success in problem solving or to learn from one's mistakes. Mediation is not just for large problems, but also for small ones that take time away from instruction and carry over into the African-American community. Dealing with small problems can prevent the need to deal with larger ones later on. Peer mediation is especially good for dealing with verbal conflicts. If the verbal conflict leads to a violent act such as a slap, then it is too late for peer mediation and an administrative referral must be pursued.

Mediators are trained in the skills of active listening, paraphrasing, "I messages," anger management, and sensitivity to diversity issues and biases. The National Association of Mediation in Education is developing standards for training students, staff, and coordinators. The average training time for students would depend on the school level, but usually takes from 12 to 20 hours.

Some schools have found peer courts and peer mentoring effective in resolving conflicts and improving behavior. Many schools are having success teaching students how to resolve conflicts without resorting to violence; instruction is done in regular classes, in counseling sessions or in other group arrangements.

The benefit of having teachers encourage the students in their classrooms to become members of the conflict-management teams must be stressed. The students who participate in the program learn social skills and how to interact with others and resolve problems caused by ethnic differences. The students who are engaged in the conflict—not teachers—should fill out the form requesting mediation. A teacher must be debriefed after each peer-mediation hearing. A list of teachers who will volunteer to serve as "debriefers" should be organized.

A counselor or clerical worker can be in charge of maintaining all peer-mediation records. A record check will prevent the same student from being pulled out of class repeatedly to act as peer mediator. Records will also reveal if the same students are being mediated too frequently. Such excesses have been a problem in some middle schools because middle-school students tend to be highly manipulative, and they quickly learn to request mediation to get out of class. It is best not to let students out of class to go to mediation the moment the conflict occurs, but to schedule them for a later time during the school day. To prevent teachers from becoming upset, students should not be allowed to miss important tests and important classes such as science labs to attend mediation.

Conflict-management teams reduce the time administrators and teachers spend dealing with inappropriate behaviors and disciplinary measures. Team members should be representative of all ethnic groups. Teachers should be scheduled to observe the teams and to participate in the selection and training of team members.

ORGANIZING A PORTFOLIO OF INTERACTIONS WITH AFRICAN-AMERICANS

To develop successful and productive interactions with African-American students and to begin to help them achieve academically requires ongoing effort over time. To organize and systematize these efforts, teachers are encouraged to keep a portfolio recording the nature of each initiative and its results. The reproducible information sheet "Multicultural Initiatives" contains a list of possible activities (see page 66). Teachers should select from the list, or from other similar activities that may occur to them, and discuss ways of carrying them out with their mentor teachers. They should then prioritize the initiatives and develop a plan for implementing each activity they have selected. These plans and all evidence relating to the execution of their plans and results should be kept in a portfolio and shared during regular conferences with the mentor teachers.

IMPLICATIONS

If teachers are to avoid becoming yet another of the many societal forces that tend to put African-American students at risk of academic and social failure, sweeping changes must be made in the school experiences provided to this significant and largely neglected ethnic group. Teachers will need training to plan and teach effective lessons to the African-American students in their classrooms. They will need the guidance of mentor teachers in designing effective lessons, and they will need the benefits of observation and feedback on the lessons they teach.

Teachers can no longer be limited to planning and teaching content. They must teach affective and social skills. Some African-Americans come from poor and dysfunctional homes where good social skills are not emphasized. Poor social skills in the classroom detract from teaching and learning.

African-American students do not learn well in chilly classroom climates. Educators must learn how to assess the climates of their schools and classrooms, and to establish and maintain supportive, welcoming climates. Modeling and extending a helping hand are powerful tools in promoting a warm and supportive multicultural climate. When African-American students see teachers caring and consistently going out of their way to help African-American students succeed in school, positive classroom climates are fostered.

ETHNIC-MINORITY-SENSITIVE LESSON PLAN (EMSLP)

Objective: To plan and teach effective lessons for classrooms with African-American students.

Directions: Use Component I of the EMSLP to develop the lesson plan. Then check to ensure that the lesson plan is suitable for classrooms with African-American students, using Component II. Responses to Components I, II, and III should be word-processed. Complete Component III only after the lesson has been taught.

COMPONENT I: DAILY LESSON PLAN OUTLINE

1. **Topic:** What is the lesson about? _____

2. **Rationale:** Why should the students learn this lesson? _____
_____

3. **Objectives:** What will the students be able to do after the lesson?
   a. _____
   b. _____
   c. _____

4. **Strategies and Activities (Methods and Procedures):** What will be done for, by, and with the students in order to reach the objectives? _____
_____
_____

5. **Materials (Equipment and Resources):** What items are needed to realize the strategies and activities?
   _____   _____   _____
   _____   _____   _____
   _____   _____   _____

6. **Plans for Differences:** How will the lesson be adapted to meet the needs of the African-American students? (Use the information in Component II to answer this question.)
_____
_____

7. **Plans for Remediation and Enrichment:** How will students be remediated (i.e., computers, independent seat work, small-group work on worksheets, peer tutoring, etc.)? How will they be enriched (i.e., interviews, projects, library research, computer simulations, etc.)? (Enrichment activities must be based on Benjamin Bloom's Taxonomy for higher-order skills and require application, analysis, evaluation, or synthesis of information.)
Remediation: _____
Enrichment: _____

8. **Evaluation:** How will students' progress based on objectives be determined (i.e., using tests, asking prepared questions, reviewing project papers, using performance checklists to evaluate student presentations, etc.)?
   _____   _____
   _____   _____

ETHNIC-MINORITY-SENSITIVE LESSON PLAN (EMSLP)

COMPONENT II: ETHNIC-MINORITY-SENSITIVE CHECKLIST

Directions: Review the lesson plan developed in Component I using the following questions.

1. Does the lesson plan show African-Americans as individuals, such as engineers, university professors, artists, governors, senators, and others, who have made important contributions to society?

   _____ yes   _____ no

   Comments: _____

   _____

2. Does the lesson portray African-Americans as individuals working, cooperating, and playing together in harmony?

   _____ yes   _____ no

   Comments: _____

   _____

3. Does the lesson plan provide a balanced representation of African-American and other groups?

   _____ yes   _____ no

   Comments: _____

   _____

4. Does the lesson plan have features that will help all students to gain knowledge and appreciation of the many contributions to our world made by members of the African-American culture?

   _____ yes   _____ no

   Comments: _____

   _____

5. Does the lesson plan provide experiences that will help build positive attitudes between students from different ethnic minority groups and promote acceptance of each ethnic minority group?

   _____ yes   _____ no

   Comments: _____

   _____

6. Does the lesson plan use words and phrases that are complimentary and honest for all ethnic minority groups?

   _____ yes   _____ no

   Comments: _____

   _____

   _____

ETHNIC-MINORITY-SENSITIVE LESSON PLAN (EMSLP)

COMPONENT III: REFLECTIONS ON STRENGTHS AND WEAKNESSES

Directions: After the lesson has been taught, the classroom teacher should use the following questions to evaluate the success of the lesson.

1. Discuss your strengths and weaknesses as a teacher during the lesson. (What worked well for you and what did not work well for you?)

_____
_____
_____
_____
_____
_____
_____
_____
_____
_____

2. Discuss what worked well for the African-American students and what did not work well for the students.

_____
_____
_____
_____
_____
_____
_____
_____
_____
_____

3. Write a plan of action to remedy any concerns you expressed in answering questions 1 and 2.

_____
_____
_____
_____
_____
_____
_____
_____
_____
_____

Ethnic-Minority Classroom Interest Inventory (EMCII)

Interest Inventory Number One

Directions: Complete each item. There are no incorrect answers.

1. If money were no object, where would you go for the perfect vacation, and what would you do while there? _____
_____

2. Who is your hero, and why? _____
_____

3. If you were a top Hollywood producer and could make a movie about anything you wanted, what would it be about? _____
Who would star in it? _____

4. If you were able to get in a time machine and go anywhere you wanted for a day, as in the movie *Back to the Future,* where would you go? _____
What would you do there? _____
_____

5. What person from history would you have enjoyed knowing? _____
Why? _____

6. If your best friend wrote a book about you, what would it be called? _____
_____

7. If you could have an article published in a popular magazine, what would be the subject?
_____
_____

8. What kind of contest would you like to win? What would you do with the prize, or the winnings? _____
_____

9. If you could have anything you wanted for your next birthday what would it be?
_____Why? _____
_____

10. Whom would you call if you had an emergency at 4 A.M.? _____
Why? _____
_____

Ethnic-Minority Classroom Interest Inventory (EMCII)

Interest Inventory Number Two

Directions: Complete each item. There are no incorrect answers.

1. Complete the sentence: I talk most when _____
_____

2. The thing I like best about myself is _____
_____.

3. I know a lot about _____
_____

4. If I could have or do anything for my birthday I would _____
_____

5. If I could be the teacher for just one day, the one thing I would change would be
_____

6. I know I can _____ better than anybody in my classroom.

7. I would like to be the first person in the world to _____
_____

8. If I could visit any place in the world, I would go to _____.
Some of the things I would do there would be _____
_____

9. If I could meet anybody in the world, I would want to meet _____
because _____

10. If I could create the perfect best friend, this is what he or she would be like: _____
_____
_____

ETHNIC-MINORITY CLASSROOM INTEREST INVENTORY (EMCII)

INTEREST INVENTORY NUMBER THREE

Directions: Complete each item. There are no incorrect answers.

1. The place I do my homework is _____.

2. The person who helps me with my homework most of the time is _____
_____

3. The thing I like best about this class is _____.

4. The thing I would change about this class is _____
_____

5. During my free time I like _____.

6. My favorite thing to do with my friends is _____
_____.

7. When I do something well, I like the teacher to _____
_____

8. I like to read books about _____

9. If I could have anything for my birthday, it would be _____
_____

10. One thing that makes me laugh is _____
In fact, a funny experience I once had was when _____
_____

ETHNIC-MINORITY CLASSROOM INTEREST INVENTORY (EMCII)

INTEREST INVENTORY NUMBER FOUR

Directions: Read the following questions aloud to students individually and enter their responses.

PERSONAL

1. Who are the people in your household? _____
_____

2. What's your favorite color? _____

3. Where do you like to go to play? _____

4. What's your favorite food? _____

5. What games do you like to play? _____

SCHOOL

1. Who reads with you at home? _____

2. My favorite thing about school is _____

3. What subject (reading, math, etc.) is your favorite? _____

4. What would you like to learn this year? _____

5. When I do something special, I think my teacher should _____
_____

NOTES

_____
_____
_____
_____

ETHNIC-MINORITY-SENSITIVE COOPERATIVE-LEARNING ACTIVITIES (EMSCLA)

Rationale: Research confirms that cooperative-learning strategies are highly effective with underachieving African-American students. As early as possible, teachers should become familiar with the strategies of cooperative learning through university courses or inservice training. When teachers implement cooperative-learning activities and lessons, they gain hands-on experiences in reinforcing the strategies of cooperative learning.

Directions: Each activity listed in the EMSCLA should be executed by the teacher with the oversight of a mentor teacher. The mentor teacher's role is to facilitate the successful completion of the EMSCLA. Use the EMSCLA with the EMSCC, which follows.

ACTIVITIES

1. Visit a nearby university library and conduct a computer search of the journal articles, conference papers, and government reports on cooperative learning (CL) that have been published within five years. This search can be narrowed with three limiting variables: (1) the age and grade level of students the teacher will be working with (elementary, middle grade, or high school); (2) urban school systems; (3) cooperative-learning strategies with African-American students. Use of these limiting variables will yield CL studies involving students that closely resemble the African-American students that the teacher will be working with.

2. Prepare a five- to ten-page review of literature synthesizing the findings, conclusions, and strategies obtained from the computer search. One section might be entitled, for example, "CL tips effective in working with urban African-American elementary fourth-graders."

3. Identify experts at a nearby teacher-training institute who conduct inservice workshops on CL and plan to participate in one. If this is not feasible, check with directors of staff development at nearby public-school districts. Most will assist teachers to gain this training.

4. Ask a mentor teacher to discuss the EMSCLA with you and assign you a standard lesson plan to revise into a brief (about 30-minute) CL lesson plan using the EMSCC.

5. Ask the mentor to review the adapted lesson plan and schedule him or her to observe your teaching of the CL lesson, looking for behaviors on the EMSCC. Teach the CL lesson with the mentor observing.

6. Meet with the mentor teacher for about 20 minutes to discuss any concerns. Solicit suggestions for improvement. Then write a summary of the strengths and weakness of the CL lesson and a plan for improving any deficiencies.

Ethnic-Minority-Sensitive Cooperative Checklist (EMSCC)

Rationale: A cooperative-learning lesson will be more effective if there is a plan to ensure that important features of CL are incorporated. A checklist of these features used to plan and teach the lesson will produce better cooperative-learning experiences for the teacher and the African-American students.

Directions: The mentor teacher and the teacher should review and discuss each step of the EMSCC to ensure that the teacher understands how to plan the CL lesson. Also employ the EMSCC in evaluating the lesson after it is taught.

Checklist Items

1. **Seating and group formation.** Before class, arrange the chairs for cooperative groups to ensure sufficient room between the chairs to circulate and offer assistance.

   Plan groups on paper to consist of three or four students each with achievement and ethnic diversity. Plan to include a high achiever, an average achiever, and a low achiever in each group. Review the planned groups and revise if necessary to ensure one or more African-Americans in each group. The African-American may be a high, average, or low achiever.

2. **Giving directions.** Students must be trained how to work together in groups; do not assume they can work together effectively without help.

   Display the directions for the CL activities on the chalkboard or on an overhead projector for the class during the entire class period, and review these orally with the class. These directions should include the following pointers, which are also available as an overhead master (see page 67):

   - Get into your group quickly.
   - Bring necessary materials with you.
   - Stay with your group until the task is finished.
   - Talk in quiet voices.
   - Listen to your partner.
   - Call your partner by name.
   - Know what your task is.

   Establish a signal to use if the noise level gets too high, such as holding up one hand or flicking the lights.

   Teachers can talk with the students about the many ways majority-culture and African-American colleagues have worked in harmony to accomplish goals in the community and at school. Students can relate to such examples as working on planning and coordinating committees for school plays, games, dances, and the school prom. Emphasize that encouraging and respecting input from all group members is critical to the achievement of group goals.

3. **Selecting the learning task.** CL activities should be short, simple, and easy while students are learning to work in groups. The materials used should reflect cultural diversity. The teacher should insist that the group's focus remain on the academic task and that students practice good social skills (Ellis & Whalen, 1992).

4. **Providing multiple opportunities for success.** Differentiate tasks for all groups to provide many ways for children to show success. If a child is a poor writer, make him the Recorder, with a checklist for gathering the group's answers or ideas. A domineering student may be designated Observer, with the rule that observers may not talk. Another child can be the Encourager, whose job is to get others to contribute. These group roles will help students to develop necessary social skills and avoid counterproductive behavior. Ensure that the African-American students have significant roles that promote participation and leadership.

5. **Learning about student interests.** Find out about the interests or hobbies of your unmotivated African-American students. Create an Interest Inventory and ask all students to fill it out. Have students interview each other about their interests.

6. **Incorporating student interests.** Find a way to incorporate the unmotivated African-American students' interests into the CL activity. Math problems using statistics from a sport may draw in a child who is a fan. A reading lesson can be developed around a famous sports figure who is a good African-American role model, such as Arthur Ashe (tennis), Michael Jordan (basketball), David Robinson (basketball), or Pele (soccer).

7. **Pointing students toward success.** To help resistant African-American students experience success at group work, identify at least one skill or talent each resistant learner possesses. Then design a group assignment so that the resistant student can use his or her skill to contribute to the group's work.

8. **Designing tasks to ensure success.** Make the task as doable as possible. Be sure instructions are clear. Give enough background information, and provide enough time. Praise individual students for contributing to their group's work. Especially watch for opportunities to praise the unmotivated African-American students and other children who traditionally receive small doses of classroom praise.

9. **Enlisting early finishers.** Use three options for early finishers: (1) Have them work on an enrichment assignment. (2) Have early finishers observe or help another group. When observing, give them something specific to look for, such as positive evidence that all group members are participating or that the group is endeavoring to address the major points associated with the CL activity. (3) Have all of the groups that are early finishers review the material (or their answers) together.

10. **Providing incentives.** Reward quiet groups and groups that work well together with something students value: praise, candy, library privileges, computer time, extra recess—whatever seems appropriate. Use donations from businesses as incentives. Ensure that some of the incentives come from African-American businesses that African-American children visit frequently and post the names of the donors in a visible place in the class. Post some incentives that highlight specific African-American cultures. These incentives can be cards, candy, posters, and certificates with African logos and names.

STEPS FOR TEACHING SOCIAL SKILLS

1. The desired social skills should be explicit and clearly defined with concrete positive and negative examples.

2. Training and practice in the skills should be built into, complement, and support the regular curriculum. Teachers should explain what the students are to do, demonstrate the skills, and have the students practice them with coaching and feedback from the teacher.

3. Opportunities should be provided for self-directed and guided application and evaluation (e.g., story telling/listening in pairs, cooperative learning, peer tutoring, and service learning).

4. Students need opportunities for making choices and decisions related to the classroom. They can actively participate in establishing class rules, weekly class meetings, and encouragement councils.

ETHNIC-MINORITY CLIMATE-BUILDING INITIATIVES (EMCBI)

1. **Expressing interest.** The teacher can be genuinely concerned about all aspects of the African-American child's life. The child must feel that the teacher is interested in his or her welfare and will stand up for him or her. Children need to feel free to discuss occurrences in their personal lives, personal feelings, and things that they enjoy doing in their free time.

2. **Keeping trust.** The teacher can consistently model honesty and sincerity. When African-American children say something in confidence, their trust should not be betrayed. All promises must be kept.

3. **Avoiding humiliation.** When there is a discipline problem with a child, the student should not be embarrassed in front of the class. Particularly, teachers should avoid backing children into a corner. This will cause even the meek student to retaliate. As much as possible, concerns about a student's classroom behavior should be discussed in private.

4. **Listening.** Teachers should be good listeners. Each child has a story to tell and wants and deserves a chance to tell it to someone who has an open mind about what occurred. Students should not be interrupted while they are telling their stories.

5. **Showing respect for property.** Teachers should model behaviors to show concern for the protection of culturally diverse students' property. An African-American child is pleased when he or she is allowed to put a prized marble, coin, or trinket on the teacher's desk for temporary safekeeping. These belongings frequently have a strong emotional value for the child. The teacher's regard for them is an indication to the African-American child that the teacher values the African-American child as a human being.

6. **Showing respect for persons.** All students want to be trusted and respected, and teachers should model such attitudes.

7. **Being outgoing.** Teachers should display an outgoing personality by smiling, expressing humor, and talking about their children, hobbies, and travels. African-American children like teachers who do things and share stories about the places they have been. Although being "pals" can be overdone, such a manner conveys the impression that a teacher accepts his or her African-American students as fellow human beings.

8. **Avoiding standoffish behavior.** The teacher should avoid appearing standoffish. An African-American child likes a teacher who will interact with him or her at football games, in the hall, and in the cafeteria.

9. **Maintaining authority.** Teachers can continue to maintain authority in the classroom even as they model behaviors reflective of being a friend to all students. African-American children want consistency, fairness, and adequate classroom control from the teacher.

CLASSROOM-CLIMATE INVENTORY—NUMBER 1

Directions: Please circle the appropriate level on the continuum that best describes our classroom.

safe	1	2	3	4	5	threatening
accepting	1	2	3	4	5	intolerant
positive	1	2	3	4	5	negative
caring	1	2	3	4	5	uncaring
recognizes my accomplishments	1	2	3	4	5	ignores my accomplishments
sets high expectations	1	2	3	4	5	sets low expectations
exciting	1	2	3	4	5	boring
makes me feel good about myself	1	2	3	4	5	makes me feel bad about myself
encourages self-expression	1	2	3	4	5	inhibits self-expression
encourages creativity	1	2	3	4	5	stifles creativity
makes me feel part of the class	1	2	3	4	5	makes me feel isolated
emphasizes the positive	1	2	3	4	5	emphasizes the negative

CLASSROOM-CLIMATE INVENTORY—NUMBER 2

Directions: Please circle the appropriate level on the continuum that best describes our classroom.

1. My teacher is prepared for class daily.

1	2	3	4	5
Always	Often	Sometimes	Seldom	Never

2. Daily class plans are flexible so as to allow for assistance in difficult academic areas.

1	2	3	4	5
Always	Often	Sometimes	Seldom	Never

3. My teacher is quick to praise my achievements.

1	2	3	4	5
Always	Often	Sometimes	Seldom	Never

4. My teacher shows concern and interest in my overall academic performance.

1	2	3	4	5
Always	Often	Sometimes	Seldom	Never

5. My teacher allows for individual differences in learning styles in the lessons.

1	2	3	4	5
Always	Often	Sometimes	Seldom	Never

6. My teacher is quick to control any behavior problems.

1	2	3	4	5
Always	Often	Sometimes	Seldom	Never

7. My teacher is considerate of students' feelings when handling discipline problems. (Does not embarrass students.)

1	2	3	4	5
Always	Often	Sometimes	Seldom	Never

8. My teacher shows respect.

1	2	3	4	5
Always	Often	Sometimes	Seldom	Never

9. The lighting in the room is appropriate for proper learning.

1	2	3	4	5
Always	Often	Sometimes	Seldom	Never

10. The overall atmosphere in the room is pleasant.

1	2	3	4	5
Always	Often	Sometimes	Seldom	Never

CLASSROOM-CLIMATE INVENTORY—NUMBER 3

Directions: Please circle the appropriate level on the continuum that best describes our classroom.

friendly	1	2	3	4	5	unfriendly
safe and orderly	1	2	3	4	5	unsafe and disorderly
conducive to learning	1	2	3	4	5	not conducive to learning
encouraging	1	2	3	4	5	discouraging
drug-free	1	2	3	4	5	not drug-free
positive	1	2	3	4	5	negative
bright and cheerful	1	2	3	4	5	dull and lifeless
quiet	1	2	3	4	5	noisy
high expectations	1	2	3	4	5	low expectations
clean	1	2	3	4	5	unclean

CLIMATE-ENHANCING STATEMENTS

Directions: Teachers should regularly find opportunities to make remarks to their colleagues similar to those listed here in order to inform them of the positive characteristics and achievements of minority students. Statements of this kind contribute to a school climate that is perceived by students as welcoming and supportive.

1. Chris is a very popular student, and others enjoy his outgoing personality. No doubt this trait will help him to achieve a high career status.

2. Frento has asked to stay after school to take part in the reteach-retest program in his civics class. By doing this he is giving up an hour of his work time at his job. His job is very important to him, so it is rewarding to see Frento place his school work before the job.

3. Tesha is doing very well in learning to control her temper. The other day a classmate made a negative remark to her, and instead of losing her temper she walked away from the situation. I am very proud of Tesha.

4. Quinzelle is always polite. He raises his hand when he has a comment or question and says "thank you" and "please." He is a very friendly student.

QUOTATIONS AND RATIONALES

The following are examples of quotations that are effective with unmotivated African-American students who have low self-esteem. The rationales may suggest the direction the discussion might take:

1. **"You may have to fight a battle more than once to win it."** (Margaret Thatcher)
    Rationale: Because of repeated failures and perceptions of failures at home and in the school, some African-American students will not attempt a new task or a task that they feel is too difficult for them. These students need to acquire the attitude of Margaret Thatcher and realize that some tasks require more effort than others. They should be helped to realize that, just because you don't succeed the first time, you should not stop trying.

2. **"You are the master of your fate."** (Anonymous)
    Rationale: Some African-American students feel they have little control over their lives and destiny. They don't see themselves as "A" students or college material. This quote helps African-American students understand that they are in control of their lives and that no one can make them do wrong. It tells them not to let others influence them in the wrong way.

3. **"Very often, failure in one thing will lead to success in another."** (Anonymous)
    Rationale: The statement tells the African-American student that failure should never be looked at as an end, but as a beginning to something new, challenging, and exciting.

4. **"A person who never makes mistakes loses lots of chances to learn something."** (Anonymous)
    Rationale: Some African-American students will sit silently in the classroom and refuse to participate in class discussions, go to the chalkboard to work problems, give class presentations, or raise their hands to answer questions. They are fearful of giving the wrong answer and being embarrassed in front of the class. This quote implies that it is okay to make mistakes. A wise person can learn from mistakes.

5. **"Success is getting up just one more time than you fall down."** (Anonymous)
    Rationale: African-American students learn that life is about getting up and falling down. This is okay, because as we continue to get up and try, we are successful.

6. **"Each day, look for the positives."** (Anonymous)
    Rationale: The statement reminds students to keep negatives out of their lives. It says, "stay away from negative people; they will destroy your self-esteem."

7. **"Be all that you can be."** (U.S. Army)
    Rationale: African-American students learn that, in order to succeed, they need to be confident in their abilities.

8. **"A mind is a terrible thing to waste."** (United Negro College Fund)
    Rationale: The statement tells African-American students that success depends on responding to challenges to the mind.

9. **"Slowly and surely wins the race."** (Aesop's Fables)
    Rationale: African-American students learn that nothing in life comes easily and one must strive patiently in all endeavors.

10. **"Nobody can be exactly like me."** (Tallulah Bankhead)
    Rationale: African-American students will recognize that each person is an individual. Thus the importance of accepting diversities in others must be emphasized and respected. For middle-school students, acceptance of self is often difficult. They must be encouraged to believe in themselves and accept the fact that each individual is unique. They should also be persuaded that the difficult period of self-questioning in adolescence is temporary and common to all young people.

11. **"You can't judge people by the way they look."** (Anonymous)
    Rationale: Many students stereotype their peers because they're more interested in being cool than in learning. This misconception prevents students from having dialogue with peers of other ethnic groups. The quote reminds students that they should look at their peers beyond first impressions.

MULTICULTURAL INITIATIVES

Directions: Teachers should discuss completion of as many of the 13 items as feasible with their mentor teachers to engender more productive teaching experiences with African-American students. Evidence of completion of the activities can be maintained in a folder and made available for mentors to evaluate.

1. Develop a resource bank listing African-American guest speakers, mentors, and tutors from various cultures. Possible sources are churches, university African-American student groups, and community organizations. Ensure that there are good role models such as Pele (soccer), Arthur Ashe (tennis), Bill Cosby (entertainment), and Harvey Gantt (architect and former mayor of Charlotte, North Carolina). Use the mentoring program to match students with adult role models of their culture and gender who are involved in the students' prospective career field.

2. Read African-American authors and literature. Contact the school librarian, a local university librarian, university English department, and a university African and African-American Studies department for help. Other sources are African-American-owned bookstores and African-American professors at major universities, especially those with degrees in English.

3. Develop and implement a role-playing exercise in which students engage in role playing that dramatizes the experience of discrimination.

4. Listen to, study, and perform music from the African-American culture. Research the biographies of artists from this culture. Sources are African-American-owned music stores and cultural centers such as the African-American Cultural Center.

5. Sample and prepare comments on the ethnic food in the cafeteria.

6. Complete research projects that deal with various ethnic groups.

7. Develop in class a multiracial peer panel to discuss a wide range of topics. Use role-playing activities to help students understand the effects of prejudice.

8. Interview African-American family members in order to develop an oral-history presentation.

9. Meet with African-American students who are signed up for standardized tests and realistically discuss the biases of these tests.

10. In the classrooms, create "culture of the month" bulletin boards that feature different cultures for at least part of each month.

11. Perform service work in the community to increase awareness of the variety of cultures in the community.

12. Coordinate a beauty contest and include African-Americans.

13. Present a case study to your mentor teacher that describes a major problem you have had involving an African-American student, parent, teacher, administrator, or community member in a particular setting. After describing and analyzing the central event and associated issues, conclude with a set of questions and learning experiences emerging from this episode.

GUIDELINES FOR COOPERATIVE GROUPS

- Get into your group quickly.

- Bring necessary materials with you.

- Stay with your group until the task is finished.

- Talk in quiet voices.

- Listen to your partner.

- Call your partner by name.

- Know what your task is.

ACTIVITIES FOR READERS OF CHAPTER TWO

1. Describe four strategies effective in finding out the interests of African-American students. Administer the Ethnic-Minority Classroom Interest Inventory (EMCII) Number One (see page 51) to all of the students in your classroom. Correlate the information collected from each of the items with each ethnic group in the classroom. For example, group the responses of all African-American students from item number one, and then group the responses of all Anglo-American students from item number one, etc. In a two-page paper, discuss how this information can be used with the Ethnic-Minority-Sensitive Checklist (Component II of the Ethnic-Minority-Sensitive Lesson Plan on page 56) to develop lesson plans that reflect the interests of the different ethnic groups in the classroom. How can this information be used as an effective source of positive reinforcement in the classroom?

2. What is cooperative learning? Discuss the advantages of cooperative learning for underachieving students in the classroom. List eight features of cooperative learning. Use the Ethnic-Minority-Sensitive Cooperative Checklist (EMSCC, see page 56) to teach a cooperative-learning lesson. Write a two-page paper reflecting on the strengths and weaknesses of the lesson. What worked well for you and what did not work well? What worked well for the students and what did not work well for the students?

3. What is peer mediation? What are the advantages for urban African-American students? Discuss some complaints teachers might have with the mediation process. What might be some typical complaints of peer mediators? Observe a mediation session in action. Interview the peer mediators and the students being mediated. In a short report, describe what happened in the observation and the interview.

SUGGESTED READINGS FOR CHAPTER TWO

Albert, L. (1990). *Cooperative discipline: Classroom management that promotes self-esteem.* Circle Pines, MN: American Guidance Service.

Brigman, G. (1993). Promoting students' self-discipline by teaching social skills and learning skills. *The National Dropout Prevention Newsletter,* 6(4), 7.

Cartledge, G., & Milburn, J.F. (1986). *Teaching social skills to children: Innovative approaches.* 2nd ed. Boston: Allyn and Bacon.

Dinkmeyer, D.C. (1989). *The parent's handbook: Systematic training for effective teaching.* Circle Pines, MN: American Guidance Service.

Elias, M.J., & Tobias, S.E. (1990). *Problem solving/decision making for social and academic success.* Washington, DC: National Education Association.

Ellis, S.S., & Whalen, S.F. (1992). Keys to cooperative learning: 35 ways to keep kids responsible, challenged, and most of all cooperative. *Instructor,* 101(6), 34-37.

Topping, K. (1988). *The peer tutoring handbook: Promoting cooperative learning.* London: Croom Helm, and Cambridge, MA: Brookline Books.

Wampler, F. (1993). Peer mediation for a new generation. *The National Dropout Prevention Newsletter,* 6(4), 4-5.

CHAPTER

Effective Interactions with Urban African-American Students

Chapter Three Objectives

After reading this chapter, readers should be able to:

Explain why mentor programs can be very effective with urban African-American male students.

Describe "cool posing" and tell how it causes cultural conflict in the classroom.

Explain why some African-American male students perceive victimization even though they have not experienced any racism.

Describe the whole-child approach as a teaching strategy.

Provide three examples of learning styles and three examples of teaching strategies that match the learning styles.

DEVELOPING AN AWARENESS OF THE AFRICAN-AMERICAN MALE CRISIS

In my workshops for public-school educators at all grade levels, majority-culture teachers and middle-class African-American teachers express frustration over their sense that they are not teaching and dealing effectively with the subcultures of African-American male students. Principals throughout the nation have reviewed standardized achievement test scores and discovered that African-American male students' scores were often lower than all other groups, including African-American females (Reglin & Harris, 1991).

In all too many cities, African-American males are not responding positively to the programs, efforts, and services of the communities, their families, and their public schools. In school, they are disciplined, expelled, and suspended at higher rates than any other group. They are more likely than Anglo-Americans to be diagnosed as mentally retarded and emotionally disturbed. African-American male students are turned off to life and to school (Comer, 1987). They feel no stake in the school—no sense of ownership or belonging.

In a review of the literature on early African-American male achievement in the elementary school, Irvine (1990) notes that, because their unique subculture is misunderstood, young African-American males are probably the most feared, least likely to be identified with, and least likely to be effectively taught. They are more likely to have nonacademic interactions with teachers and more likely to be isolated socially and academically from Anglo-American students.

A noted colleague of mine, James Comer of Yale University, eloquently addressed this situation in February 1991 in Savannah, Georgia, at the Second Annual Conference on Youth At Risk. Dr. Comer contended that America must move rapidly in implementing solutions to the situation he referred to as the "African-American Male Crisis." If it is not attended to quickly and properly, he said, the African-American Male Crisis could escalate to a point at which a solution would be almost impossible. Dr. Comer is correct; we are nearing the point of no return.

Comer found that many professional educators responded to these children by controlling or attempting to control them, or by communicating low expectations of them. This caused the students either not to respond or to respond in ways that made matters worse. Evidence that these traditional approaches are not working is manifested in the following statistics:

(1) By the year 2000, up to 70 percent of African-American males may be in prisons.

(2) Sixty percent of African-American children live in poverty.

(3) Fifty-eight percent of African-American children live with single parents.

(4) There is a shortage of positive African-American male role models.

What are the implications of these statistics?

BY THE YEAR 2000, UP TO 70 PERCENT OF AFRICAN-AMERICAN MALES MAY BE IN PRISONS.

African-Americans are the largest ethnic minority group in the United States, about 12 percent of the population. However, the plight of the African-American male in America is pronounced. He has become an endangered species (Wright, 1991). Between 1973 and 1986, average real earnings for African-American males ages 20 to 24 fell by 50 percent. In 1986 real earnings for African-American men averaged $7,447. African-American males constitute six percent of the population, but make up 40 percent of the prison population. The percentages are higher in the Deep South.

If the trend continues, by the year 2000, it is conceivable that up to 70 percent of the African-American males in this country may be either killed, awaiting trial, imprisoned, or addicted to drugs (Commission on Minority Participation in Education and American Life, 1988). The leading cause of death among African-American males between the ages of 15 and 24 is homicide.

Sixty percent of African-American children live in poverty.

Nearly 60 percent of all African-American children live below the poverty line (Honing, 1990). In 1990, over 30 percent of students in public schools—some 12 million—were from minority groups (Quality Education for Minorities Projects, 1990). A 1988 report by the American Council on Education and the Education Commission of the States project that in the year 2000 well over one-third of the national population will be of African-American and/or Hispanic descent, while about 42 percent of the school population will be of similar ethnicity.

In 1990, 13 percent of African-American youths between the ages of 16 and 24 dropped out of high school, compared to nine percent of Anglo-American youths (U.S. Bureau of the Census, 1992). African-American students are disproportionately represented in low-ability groups and seldom tracked into college preparatory courses. Despite being in the minority, African-American males constitute the largest proportion of students in special-education classes.

Fewer than 30 percent of all African-American students take courses that prepare them for a four-year college. Of all African-American males in college, 43 percent enroll in two-year colleges, but only 10 percent make the transition to four-year colleges. Among African-American males who did enroll in Atlanta-area colleges in 1986-1987, 77 percent dropped out or were held back during their first year (Ascher, 1992).

Fifty-eight percent of African-American children live with single parents.

A large number of African-American boys are from single-parent homes headed by their mothers, guardians, older sisters, aunts, or grandmothers, or some other female caregiver. Children from single-parent families are more likely to show behavioral problems such as absenteeism, tardiness, truancy, inefficient study habits at home, and disruptive classroom behavior (Reglin, 1993b).

Recently released data from the U.S. Bureau of the Census (1992) show that the percentage of African-American children living with just one parent increased from 31.8 percent in 1970 to 45.8 percent in 1980, and had risen as high as 58 percent as of March 1991. Of the 5.8 million African-American children living with one parent, the vast majority (5.5 million) live with their mothers, the report said. The probability of a child from a single-parent family ending up in poverty is six times greater than that of a child from a two-parent family.

Adults other than a child's parents are taking on significant child-rearing roles (Reglin, 1993b). In the last 20 years, the percentage of African-American children being raised by grandparents has risen from 3.2 percent to 12.5 percent—one in eight (Edwards & Young, 1992). Many children in the middle schools are having babies. Households with African-American children under 18 years of age commonly include foster parents, extended families, children living with other relatives, adoptive parents, or reconstituted and blended families.

THERE IS A SHORTAGE OF POSITIVE MALE MENTORS AND ROLE MODELS.

African-American male children suffer a veritable penury of positive male mentors and positive male role models in their everyday surroundings. If they attend Sunday school, they are taught by females, and females are usually their teachers in grades kindergarten through four as well. Furthermore, if the principal is female, a female teacher sends them to a female principal for reprimand and/or punishment when they get in trouble. Their inappropriate behavior is reported to a female head of household. All of the legitimate mentors, role models, and authority figures in the lives of most of these boys for the first eight to nine years of their lives are females.

The flight of middle-class African-Americans from inner-city neighborhoods and the high incidence of unemployment among African-Americans who remain cause African-American male students to suffer from a lack of appropriate, mainstream male models at home and in their communities (Ascher, 1992). T. Prince (1990), who runs a mentoring program at Morehouse College in Atlanta for African-American male elementary school students, pointed out that more than 40 percent of these children do not see their fathers at all in a typical year. Only one in five sleeps in a father's home in a typical month. In short, more and more of these children simply do not know what it means to have a father. Instead, African-American boys are surrounded by an overabundance of negative images of African-American men.

The negative images of African-Americans on the streets, in schools, and in the media have wrought serious harm to the self-esteem of African-American male students. Young students see few alternative positive images or models. Moreover, the pervasive negative image of African-Americans influences teachers, who complete the vicious circle by doubting the abilities of their African-American male students.

In spite of these depressing data, teachers have the power to turn this dire situation around and help young African-Americans students feel that the school is their place—a place that can make a difference for themselves and their lives. The remaining pages of this chapter will outline a plan of action that will produce better experiences and greater achievement when working with African-American male students.

A Plan of Action for Working with African-American Male Students

The blueprint for action presented here is designed to provide urban African-American males with experiences of success and to reinforce these successes. The major thrust of the plan is to replace the failure and frustration so common among African-American male students with ample opportunities for successful activities and the positive feelings these engender. When their time and energy is filled with constructive, morale- and esteem-enhancing occupations, they soon renounce the previous pattern of attention-seeking, ego-satisfying behavior with which they have tried to fill the void of positive relationships in their lives.

All educators involved in the success of African-American male students must be encouraged and trained to innovate. They will find that innovative activities organized in the following six areas are particularly effective. The six areas are listed here. Each will be discussed in the pages that follow.

- Dealing with African-American Male Subculture ("Cool Posing")
- Dealing with Racism and Perceptions of Victimization
- Emphasizing the Whole Child
- Building Self-Esteem
- Cross-Age and Peer Tutoring
- Learning-Styles Instruction

Dealing with African-American Male Subculture ("Cool Posing")

Hale-Benson (1986), in her study of African-American culture and history, contends that the culture transmitted to African-American children through their families and churches stands in sharp contrast to the dominant culture's approach to education, which young African-Americans encounter in integrated schools. Recent research studies (Owens, 1993; Majors & Billson, 1992; & Reglin & Harris, 1991) discuss a new subculture that has become dominant among African-American male students and that causes much cultural conflict in the school building. This conflict adversely affects African-American male children's adjustment and learning.

This urban African-American male subculture stems from a significant focus on popular sports figures, popular entertainers (particularly rap groups), and interactions with the peer group. The peer group assumes the role of the extended family and becomes a major factor in reinforcing the values and behaviors that make up this subculture.

Much of the subculture obtained from sports, music videos, entertainment (rap groups), peer groups, and TV are attempts to fill voids in the students' lives. To fill these voids, they desperately attempt to bond themselves with a peer group and to establish meaningful relationships. These children need many adults in their lives with whom to establish positive connections, particularly positive male adult role models.

75

The simple truth is that many urban African-American male students are no longer receiving nurturing from the adults who traditionally provided caring and concern and a sense of being special. These were the adults in the immediate family, extended family, church, and community. Many were positive African-American adult male role models. Now different values, obtained from other sources, are manifesting themselves as a subculture and carrying themselves over into the school building. Oftentimes, this subculture creates conflict between educators and students.

The typical classroom in America is led by an Anglo-American female, usually in her late 30s (Johnson, 1990). Teacher-training programs have failed to provide these teachers with adequate teacher-education experiences (both curricular and clinical/field) that would equip them with the tools to effectively understand the new subculture of African-American males. Typical African-American male behavior in the classroom, such as wolfing, pimping, and jiving, is viewed (by Anglo-American females) as hostile, threatening, and inappropriate. According to Owens (1993), there are many more subculture behaviors that may conflict with school policy and thus cause cultural conflict, but which are important to the African-American male child because they give him a sense of dignity, self-worth, and identity. These behaviors are marked by wearing certain dress, sometimes in a particular manner, including the following features:

(1) Hats in the school building

(2) Hats backward or turned to the side

(3) Heavy coats in the building

(4) Ear rings in the ears

(5) Pants that are baggy (loose fitting) and hanging off the "hips" instead of being secured at the waist with a belt

(6) T-shirts with obscene language

(7) T-shirts that represent the latest slogans, both those quoted in the media and those popular among celebrities

White-Hood (1990) believes African-American males have created a rare subculture with unique language patterns, dress, attire, music, values, and ways of behaving. Historically, these cultural expressions have led to much misunderstanding. One such cultural expression is "cool posing." Wiley (1990) has defined cool posing as a coping mechanism by which African-American males deal with the bitterness of racism in this society. He further explained that cool posing is an ego-booster (self-esteem) comparable to that which Anglo-American males find through work, school, media, support networks, and social surroundings. African-American males are not likely to have opportunities to fulfill such traditional roles of manhood as bread-winner, provider, and protector, and cool posing provides them with an alternative way of establishing their identity.

Majors & Billson (1992) see cool posing as a mask to hide many of the problems the urban African-American male child confronts on a daily basis. The cool pose becomes a camouflage to disguise his hurt, but is often misread by urban educators as aggressive and irresponsible behavior.

Seven strategies developed from my research and personal experience will help educators deal with the subcultures of African-American male students. These strategies range from gaining awareness of the characteristics of the culture to methods for developing more positive interactions with the students and their families. They are listed in the reproducible information sheet "Seven Strategies for Dealing with Young Urban African-Americans" (see page 83).

DEALING WITH RACISM AND PERCEPTIONS OF VICTIMIZATION

Unfortunate but true, African-American male children are informed by adults in their homes and communities that the economic and social problems faced by African-American people are the result of racism by an Anglo-American society. Conversations about being victims echo through the lives of African-American children. They begin to start thinking of themselves as victims at an early age, even though they may not have experienced any racism. These children start to believe that working hard in school to get good grades will not lead to a successful future in their adult lives because of the inequities in society.

African-American youth learn early that an Anglo-American male with a high school diploma or a college degree will make more than an African-American male with similar credentials. Motivation to study is affected when young people see that it is possible to earn more by selling drugs than by a acquiring a college education that may be unaffordable and may not produce a job. Michelson (1990) illustrated this attitude.

> *Larry, a young African-American man enrolled at UCLA, walked into a local bank and spotted Antoine, a friend from high school, who was working as a security guard. They exchanged greetings. Antoine asked Larry how he was doing. Larry complained that he was exhausted from working full time to support carrying a full load at UCLA. "Why are you working so hard?" laughed Antoine. "You are gonna end up as a security guard like me, but you'll lose your hair sooner."*

Even in the absence of peer pressure, looking at life from the perspective of victimization will prevent African-American male children from adopting serious academic attitudes and persevering in their schoolwork (Ogbu, 1990). Many have also internalized the belief that to take academic efforts seriously is to act Anglo-American, but they are unassured of acceptance by Anglo-Americans even if they succeed in learning to act Anglo-American.

The relationship between African-Americans and those who control the schools does not help to promote academic achievement among African-American children. African-Americans have acquired a basic distrust for the public schools and for school personnel and believe that they are provided with an inferior education.

Ogbu (1990) stated that the legacy of distrust among African-Americans may take more than high teacher expectations to address. Many African-American adults feel that African-American children, particularly African-American male children, are adversely affected by being labeled learning disabled, which results in the disproportionate channeling of African-American students into special-education classes. Teachers can minimize their African-American male students' feelings of victimization by adopting the techniques listed in "Seven Strategies for Overcoming a Sense of Victimization" (see page 84).

EMPHASIZING THE WHOLE CHILD

African-American male students perform better in the classroom when teachers teach to the cognitive, affective, and social dimensions of the students. Teaching the whole child demands that teachers internalize the fact that they do not merely teach subjects, they teach people. Teachers must model superior interpersonal skills and establish a good rapport with the student. Six strategies are suggested (see "Six Strategies for Emphasizing the Whole Child," page 85). These strategies involve conveying sincere interest in the child and all aspects of his or her life, not just the academic side.

The whole-child approach takes the entire person into account rather than merely parts of the person. Many African-American males are in low-track and remediation programs. These programs do not treat the whole child. Tracking systems or ability grouping perpetuates failure by reminding African-American male students that they are not as good as other students. Tracking destroys self-esteem and reinforces low achievement. Unfortunately, it is profoundly ingrained in most public schools.

Remediation is based on the assumption that identified deficiencies in a person can be repaired, just as an inoperative motor is repaired. That is, schools measure what needs to be repaired and provide remedial instruction in the subject matter (Garton, 1984).

Teachers should come to realize that low-track classes and remedial programs will not significantly increase achievement for these students and should be avoided and opposed. African-American male students must be heterogeneously grouped in classrooms where all students are judged capable of learning. In this heterogeneous grouping, the whole-child approach needs be the dominant teaching strategy.

Numerous research studies have demonstrated that the key to raising the achievement level of African-American male students is to raise their self-esteem. Teaching the whole child is one of the means of increasing self-esteem. With this approach, African-American male students—and all students—are encouraged and nurtured as people, not as repositories of information. Teachers work with students' attitudes, self-concepts, and personal problems. They endeavor to make sense of their home lives. They become aware of the adults and peers in the students' environment who affect the students positively and negatively. The total environment of African-American male children must be of paramount concern to augment their achievement.

BUILDING SELF-ESTEEM

When African-American male students feel better about themselves, they do better in school. The simple fact is, though, that many African-American males today are not receiving enough positive nurturing attention from adults, either at home or at school. This is causing more and more of these students to have low levels of self-esteem. Three strategies (Canfield, 1990) that promote high self-esteem are suggested (see "Three Self-Esteem Strategies," page 86).

One of the three strategies utilizes a set of four excellent role-playing activities shared by veteran teachers and field-tested using teachers in my summer teacher institute. These are designed to assist low-achieving students in eliminating negative statements or thoughts and replacing them with positive ones by focusing on positive self-esteem statements. These role plays will help students overcome habits of negative thoughts and statements. The activities have been found effective in enhancing the self-esteem of low-achieving urban African-American male students. The four role-playing self-esteem activities, described on pages 87-89, are

• The Canceler
• The Puppet Theater
• Overcoming Killer Statements and Gestures
• The Plain White Paper Incident

CROSS-AGE AND PEER TUTORING

Tutoring can be before, during, and after class. All tutors should be trained. An example of cross-age tutoring is having fourth- and fifth-grade students tutoring first- and second-grade students. A significant amount of research demonstrates the positive effects of tutoring on self-esteem, attitudes, and achievement, as well as desirable outcomes for both tutors and tutees. Tutoring induces both antisocial and underachieving students to take their work more seriously. Cross-age tutoring is more effective when African-American male students play the role of tutor to younger students.

African-American male students can relate directly to those who are not far in age and experience from themselves. The younger students may learn more from the tutor than from their teachers because of personality clashes or communication problems with the teachers or because the tutor may use language or examples that are more readily understood by the tutee.

Tutors who are close in age to tutees may remember their own difficulties with the materials. If possible, coordinate cross-age tutoring (older children working with younger children) and peer tutoring (students are tutored by classmates) to be accomplished in cooperative-learning groups. This will prevent many problems, such as tutees being afraid of losing face before their peers, or tutees believing they know more than the tutors.

LEARNING-STYLES INSTRUCTION

Goodlad (1984) found that teachers tend to teach the way they prefer to learn. As a result, the different learning styles and needs of many African-American male students tend to go unmet. These findings hold true from kindergarten through the university, with the variety of teaching styles and strategies represented diminishing the higher one goes through school. Goodlad (1984) found lecture to be the primary teaching style about 70 percent of the time between the fourth grade and the beginning of high school. This figure mounted even further in high school and beyond.

Both teaching and learning styles can be categorized as either field-independent or field-sensitive. Field-independent teachers encourage independent student achievement and competition among students. Field-sensitive teachers are more interpersonally oriented and prefer situations that allow them to use personal conversational techniques. Similarly, field-sensitive students perform better in social situations such as group work. Many African-American male students are field-sensitive.

Hale-Benson (1986) states that African-American students have a learning style that is different from that of Anglo-American students, one that is unique to the African-American culture. She reports that African-American students are more feeling- and people-oriented and more proficient at nonverbal communication than Anglo-American children.

Hale-Benson found that the core of the African-American cultural style is a tendency to respond to things in terms of the whole picture instead of its parts. A significant number of researchers supporting learning-styles instruction contended that the emphasis of traditional education has been upon molding and shaping African-American male children so that they can be fitted into an educational process designed for Anglo-American middle-class children.

The Myers-Briggs Type Indicator (MBTI), a learning-style instrument that provides bias-free learning-style profiles, was given to students in five high school science classes in a county with one of the highest rates of both poverty and African-Americans of any county in North Carolina (Melear & Pitchford, 1992). This study found a significant difference in the learning styles of African-Americans and Anglo-Americans. It found that African-Americans, particularly African-American males, were Extraverts (E), Sensing (S), Thinking (T), and Perceiving (P). The conclusion was that the best learning environment for students with these preferences should provide

(1) opportunities for talking

(2) learning experiences which are mostly concrete and related to real-life situations and which are practical

(3) logical learning experiences

(4) flexibility in both completion and location of tasks

Effective programs for African-American male students that capitalize on learning-styles research include six features:

(1) Cooperative Learning (which gives students more opportunity to talk among themselves)

(2) Data gathering and analysis of real-world problems (concrete and logical experiences)

(3) Less emphasis on one right answer and one teaching format (less lecture and more variety in instruction)

(4) Activities that enable the students to become actively involved in the pursuit of a concrete, tangible goal

(5) Activities that are related to the students' own experiences and culture

(6) Activities that the students help to plan and carry out

Teachers can best accommodate the varied learning styles in the classroom by incorporating variety into the learning situations and learning media of their students. For example, some students should be permitted to work with other students, with teachers, with other adults, with multimedia, and cooperatively on computers. Overall achievement of African-American male students is enhanced by a variety in learning media such as

- cassette tapes
- videotapes
- lectures
- discussions
- records
- radio
- stereo
- television

These strategies and materials are also listed on the reproducible information sheet "Strategies and Materials Effective with Varied Learning Styles" (see page 90).

School officials should encourage teachers to read as much as possible on learning styles and should seek funding for several teachers to attend workshops and then train their colleagues in this promising method for enhancing the achievement of all students. Learning-style inventories are usually very easy to administer and score. They should be given to all students in the school during the first two weeks of class. The time it takes for students to complete an inventory ranges from 20 to 90 minutes.

"Learning Styles and Teaching Strategies" (see page 91) describes some different learning styles and appropriate teaching strategies to accommodate them. They reveal that appropriate teaching strategies can be quickly and easily implemented to match with the different learning styles of students.

Success for African-American male students is facilitated when a variety of instructional strategies is used. Research and my personal experience show that these students emphatically agree that lectures are their least preferred learning method, yet lecture is the most common instructional mode used by regular classroom teachers. Many of these students are not auditory learners and find lectures boring and difficult to follow. Achievement and motivation increase significantly when such activities as individual work, small-group activities, class discussions, and audio presentations are used.

IMPLICATIONS

In 1987, the Council of Chief State School Officers published *Children At Risk: The Work of the States*. The document stated that more African-American male children are entering school from poverty households and single-parent households. Historically, many middle-class minority-culture and majority-culture teachers have not done well with these children.

To improve learning for these students, teachers can use vital instructional strategies such as learning styles and cooperative learning. Social-skills instruction and positive reinforcement techniques are excellent classroom practices.

Saracho and Gerstl (1992) suggest that ethnic minority groups, independent of socioeconomic status, display characteristic patterns of thinking styles that are different from one another. Members of a specific culture are socialized within a matrix of cultural history, adaptive approaches to reality, and behavior patterns. Teachers can reflect this important research in their instructional practices.

New technologies significantly increase the learning of underachieving African-American males. The technologies must be wholeheartedly adopted by teachers. Computers provide immediate feedback with the attendant motivational advantages. In addition, interactive videodisc/computer technology mixes visual, tactile, and listening modes of learning, and offers a nonjudgmental, private environment in which African-American male students can test their own thinking at their own speed.

When used as a teaching tool, computers can be invaluable in individualizing and accelerating student learning. Determining appropriate software to use with underachieving African-American male students and identifying the most effective mix of instructional strategies should be part of the teaching repertoire of all K-12 teachers.

Teachers should continue to provide experiences reflective of good classroom instruction throughout the public-school life of these children. They will have to be observed, videotaped, and critiqued by school administrators and their peers implementing this instruction on a frequent basis. The end result will be positive academic performance for African-American male students.

Seven Strategies for Dealing with Young Urban African-Americans

(1) **Developing awareness.** Professional educators should seek opportunities for inservice training and individual research in current books and educational journals to gain awareness of African-American male students' values, preparation, and experiences that arise from their subculture, where they are acceptable. Administrators should provide incentives for the development of this awareness.

(2) **Getting acquainted with peers.** African-American children often live in two worlds, that of the dominant society and that of their own cultural group. They are sometimes confused as to where they belong and where they want to be. Peers, to whom they may feel a very strong attachment, are often more influential than their parents or guardians. Teachers must become familiar with the backgrounds of the peers with whom their African-American male students frequently associate at school. Much can be learned by being aware of the peers African-American male students interact with on a frequent basis.

(3) **Making school culture explicit.** The assumptions, expectations, and ways of doing things in school—in short, its culture—must be made explicit to African-American male students through explanation and modeling at every opportunity (Knapp, Turnbull, & Shields, 1990).

As the school leader and climate setter, the principal must be proactive in convincing all personnel on the school grounds to model behaviors supportive of academic learning at all times. The principal must convince both minority-culture and majority-culture personnel alike that the primary mission of the school is to help children learn. Custodians, teacher aides, substitute teachers, clerks, cafeteria workers, assistant principals, volunteer workers, teachers, and all other school employees are important in this endeavor.

(4) **Role playing.** Teachers can engage in role-playing activities enacting cool posing to develop a sense of the social problems that African-American male students are trying to camouflage. The role play will allow teachers to experience the many obstacles African-American male students face in the community and the school.

(5) **Conveying warmth.** All persons in the learning environment of the students must be warm, outgoing, flexible, and supportive so that the students can have confidence and trust in their teachers' innate abilities.

(6) **Conveying trust.** All educators and school personnel must convey a genuine belief in the ultimate good of every human being and a profound desire to communicate with the youth and their parents.

(7) **Interactions with families.** Frequent interactions and visits with parents or guardians are imperative. Examples include home visits, parent-teacher conferences, phone calls, and interactions in African-American community organizations. These activities will allow educators to become more sensitized to life on the other side of the fence.

SEVEN STRATEGIES FOR OVERCOMING A SENSE OF VICTIMIZATION

(1) **Cooperative learning.** Cooperative-learning (CL) groups that include both African-American and Anglo-American students should be utilized frequently to help all students achieve academic goals, develop good human-relations skills, and increase opportunities for education in character development.

(2) **Role models.** Successful African-American male role models should be invited into the classroom as mentors, tutors, and guest speakers.

(3) **Positive reinforcement.** Positive reinforcement—"catching them being good"—that notices and praises positive behaviors is more effective than always remarking on the negative behaviors.

(4) **Emphasizing the positive.** The talents and strengths of the students should be identified and celebrated in front of their peers and parents.

(5) **Avoiding labels.** Students should not be labeled anything except human beings.

(6) **Avoiding tracking.** Tracking students into low-ability classes should be minimized. Alternative strategies that are usually much more effective include mastery learning, outcome-based education, and cooperative learning. Curriculum should be individualized as much as possible.

(7) **Modeling.** An attitude of caring and genuine concern for the problems of all students should be conveyed by all staff members, who should treat students as they would like to be treated.

SIX STRATEGIES FOR EMPHASIZING THE WHOLE CHILD

(1) **Expressing concern.** Educators should show empathy for the personal problems of students and model respect and genuine sincerity at all times.

(2) **Respecting privacy.** Conferences with students about academic and discipline problems should be conducted privately, and the conversation should begin and end with positive information.

(3) **Listening.** Children need adults with good listening skills who don't interrupt them while they are trying to tell their side of the story.

(4) **Troubleshooting.** Teachers can gain the trust of their students when they help them solve their personal and immediate concerns, although trust-building requires patience and time to build.

(5) **Reaching out.** School personnel should not be standoffish with these students but deliberately seek positive interactions with them, particularly at school events and in the presence of parents and friends.

(6) **Avoiding embarrassment.** Students should never be embarrassed or pushed into a corner in the classroom. The most mild-mannered student will usually fight back when humiliated in front of his or her friends. Should an ugly scene occur, the teacher may lose the respect of the other African-American students.

Three Self-Esteem Strategies

I. Teach the African-American male students to focus on the positive.

Rationale: In order to feel successful, a person has to have experienced success. Many students, because they feel they have never done anything successful, need to be coached. Often they equate "success" with winning a medal, getting rich, becoming class president, being a successful rap singer, or becoming the next Michael Jordan.

Procedure: As a class activity, have the students draw and share their past achievements. With some probing and discussion, assist the students in identifying some successful aspects of their lives they have not recognized before.

II. Establish classroom support groups.

Rationale: It's possible for some African-American male students to come to school for a whole day and never once be the center of positive attention. Support groups help focus positive attention on the student.

Procedure: Ask the student to find a partner and then give the two of them three minutes to talk about any positive topic they may be interested in. Examples of topics to suggest include

What movie did you see last? Did you enjoy it? Why?

If you could become President of the United States for one day, what changes would you make and why?

Students learn that it is a positive, healing experience to talk about their feelings, and they begin to bond with their fellow students.

III. Teach the African-American male students to monitor self-talk.

Rationale: Each of us thinks 50,000 thoughts per day, and many of them are about ourselves. Because of bad experiences, many African-American male students think negative thoughts.

Procedure: Conduct brief (five-minute) activities designed to replace negative thoughts with positive self-talk: "I can't dance," "I'm not smart," "I don't like my face" are countered by "I can learn to do anything I want," "I am smart," "I love and accept myself the way I am." Students are taught to say, "Cancel, cancel" when they hear themselves or another person saying something negative about them and to replace the negative remark with a positive one. Also, whenever others put them down, they should repeat the following "antidote" sentence: "No matter what you say or do to me, I'm still a worthwhile person."

Then guide students in the following four role-playing activities:

1. THE CANCELER

Appropriate Age Group:

> Upper Elementary School, Middle School, and High School

Procedure:

> Students work in triads. They list 15 common negative thoughts and statements they hear other students make. For each item they write a positive counterstatement. Students are assigned roles: positive student, negative student, and canceler. The negative student directs statements to the positive student. The canceler says "Cancel, cancel" and the positive student responds with a self-affirmative statement. Students switch roles after every fifth statement.

Example:

> Negative student: "You missed that easy math problem. You must be stupid."
> Canceler: "Cancel, cancel," or "Stop," or "Not true."
> Positive student: "It was only one problem and his opinion doesn't matter anyway."

Conclusion:

> Ask students to discuss the purpose of the role play. The teacher defines self-esteem and summarizes the activity.

2. THE PUPPET THEATER

Appropriate Age Group:

> Lower Elementary School (grades 1 and 2)

Procedure:

> The teacher and the teacher assistant should run the Theater. Two furry, kid-friendly puppets are introduced. They demonstrate a situation in which the first makes a mistake and the second calls him (or her) names.

Example:

> Farley says, "Freddy can't color in the lines. He's a baby." Freddy gets upset and begins to cry. An adult-looking, non-furry puppet enters and asks each of the other two, "How do you feel when someone says things like that to you?"

> The third puppet then asks children in the audience to tell of times something like this has happened to them. After they have shared experiences, the third puppet goes on to introduce the concept of self-talk to the children.

> The same beginning scenario with the two furry puppets is replayed, but this time with examples of appropriate responses to bad remarks. For example, Freddy says to himself, "Stop—I'm not a baby." Then he says to Farley, "It hurts my feelings when you call me names. Everyone makes mistakes sometimes. Do you know a way to do it better?"

Conclusion:

> Children are paired and practice self-talk and expressing positive feedback to negative comments. Teachers should also reinforce the message that negative comments are hurtful.

3. Overcoming Killer Statements and Gestures

Appropriate Age Group:

Upper Elementary School, Middle School, and High School

Rationale:

Each of us has many feelings, thoughts, and creative behaviors that are killed off by other people's negative comments, physical gestures, and other put-downs. Some killer statements that are often used, even by teachers, include

- "We don't have time for that now."
- "That's a stupid idea. You know that's impossible."
- "You're really weird."
- "Are you crazy?" "Retarded?" "Kidding me?" "Serious?"
- "Only girls/boys do that."
- "Wow, he's strange, man, really strange."
- "That stuff's for sissies."

Procedure:

Introduce the concept of killer statements and gestures to the students. Tell them that they're going to be social-science researchers for the day. Ask them to keep a record of all the killer statements they hear in school, at lunch, at home, and at play. During the next class period, elicit one killer statement and volunteers to role-play the situation in which it was heard. As a class, develop a list of positive thoughts that could be used to negate the killer statement. After the list is generated, ask the student playing the respondent to hold up a mirror to himself/herself and begin the self-talk practice as a reinforcement.

Example:

Student-to-student: "You're really weird."

Student respondent (self-talk): "I'm not weird. It's O.K. to be different. I am greater than weird. I'm special and I know it."

Divide the class into heterogeneous cooperative groups. Ask each group to create a master list of killer statements and positive mental thoughts for each one. Allow groups the opportunity to practice self-talk through role play. Collect the master lists and devise a journal for students to keep on hand as a reference tool for future use.

Ask the students to stand up. When the teacher says "Go!" they are to say or shout all the killer statements that they have collected. The teacher tells them to use all the killer statements, gestures, and sounds they want to. They can shout at the air, their desk, chair, or whatever else feels comfortable to rid themselves of the negative effects forever.

Conclusion:

Present the journals to the students, discussing the purpose of self-talk in enhancing self-esteem.

4. THE PLAIN WHITE PAPER INCIDENT

Appropriate Age Group:

Upper Elementary School, Middle School, and High School

Purpose:

To show students how negative comments affect self-esteem and how self-talk can deflect negative comments.

Supplies:

Two sheets of plain white 8.5" x 11" paper labeled "Self-Esteem."

Procedure:

1. The teacher holds a sheet of paper in one hand and explains that each person starts out with self-esteem, but each time a negative comment is heard self-esteem is damaged. To demonstrate this, the teacher begins making derogatory comments about her- or himself. After each comment, he or she tears a piece off of self-esteem. Comments continue until the paper—and the self-esteem—is destroyed.

2. The teacher asks students what they can do to prevent their self-esteem from being destroyed. Students brainstorm ideas and a recorder lists them on the board or overhead. The teacher leads students to bring up self-talk.

3. The teacher reviews the suggestions with the class. Suggestions are deleted if found unworkable. Workable suggestions are discussed and the teacher explains self-talk.

4. The teacher holds a second sheet of paper labeled "Self-Esteem." The teacher makes derogatory comments about him- or herself and asks students for help in countering each comment with self-talk. The teacher tears paper when a comment is made but repairs it with tape when self-talk is used.

Conclusion:

The teacher has students describe the condition of the paper before negative comments, after negative comments with no self-talk, and after negative comments with self-talk. Descriptions should then be related, through discussion, to self-esteem in individuals and how self-talk can help people maintain self-esteem.

STRATEGIES AND MATERIALS EFFECTIVE WITH VARIED LEARNING STYLES

Learning-styles research has shown that the following strategies can be used effectively with classes containing students with varied learning styles:

(1) Cooperative learning (which gives students more opportunity to talk among themselves)

(2) Data gathering and analysis of real-world problems (concrete and logical experiences)

(3) Less emphasis on one right answer and one teaching format (less lecture and more variety in instruction)

(4) Activities that enable the students to become actively involved in the pursuit of a concrete, tangible goal

(5) Activities that are related to the students' own experiences and culture

(6) Activities that the students help to plan and carry out

The following materials and learning media are also effective in enhancing the learning of African-American and other students with alternative learning styles:

- cassette tapes
- videotapes
- lectures
- discussions
- records
- radio
- stereo
- television

LEARNING STYLES AND TEACHING STRATEGIES

Learning Style. Preference for high mobility

Appropriate Teaching Strategies. Establish bulletin boards as learning centers that allow students to stand while completing a task. Reading tasks could require students to move from one place to another before the task is complete.

Learning Style. Tactile

Appropriate Teaching Strategies. Activities involving touching-to-learn should be effective. Allow students to write summaries and create graphic organizers to enhance comprehension and retention of text. The discovery method, experimentation, and model building are effective teaching strategies.

Learning Style. Kinesthetic

Appropriate Teaching Strategies. Allow students to drum their fingers on the desk or swing their feet while reading. Plan field trips and visits.

ACTIVITIES FOR READERS OF CHAPTER THREE

1. Why is it that some African-American male students think like victims at an early age, even though they might not have experienced any racism? Discuss five strategies teachers can use to minimize feelings of victimization.

2. Explain the three strategies teachers can use to promote high self-esteem. Design a five-minute role-playing activity that will teach urban African-American male students to monitor self-talk. Ensure that the activity is appropriate for the grade level of your students.

SUGGESTED READINGS FOR CHAPTER THREE

Ogbu, J.U. (1992). Understanding cultural differences and school learning. *Educational Libraries,* 16(3), 7-11.

Owens, I.L. (1993). Understanding the young Black male client in SAPs. *Student Assistance Journal,* 6(3), 20-34.

Reglin, G.L., & Harris, S. (1991). *Effectively addressing the needs of middle school and high school at-risk Black males in solving the problems of youth at risk.* Lancaster, PA: Technomic.

Saracho, O.N., & Gerstl, C.K. (1992). Learning differences among at-risk minority students. In Waxman, H.C., Felix, J.E., Anderson, L.E., and Baptiste, H.P.: *Students at risk in at-risk schools.* Newbury Park, CA: Corwin Press, pp. 105-135.

White-Hood, M. (1990). Unforgettable: The Black male student in our schools. *Early Adolescence,* 5(2), 11-12.

C H A P T E R

Involving African-American Parents in Their Children's Education

Chapter Four Objectives

After reading this chapter, readers should be able to:

Identify three reasons why some urban African-American parents do not get involved in the school.

Identify at least three strategies effective in improving communications with the parents.

Explain the purpose of the parent-support plan.

Discuss school-initiated strategies to improve the home-school-community connections and state the role of the school and the role of the community in each strategy.

State four ways the community can assist the school with male mentors and male role models.

OBSTACLES TO INVOLVEMENT

The myth that urban African-American parents don't want to get involved in school is prevalent in public education. However, my personal experience supports research that reveals that all parents care about the education of their children. Schools can be innovative in reaching out to parents and encouraging their involvement. Comer (1987) claims, "The presence of African-American parents and the support they offer decrease conflict and apathy in the school." African-American parents do not have to be well-educated to make a difference in school.

Research shows a strong positive relationship between minority-parent involvement and minority-student achievement (Walberg, 1984). In addition to the positive relationship between parent-involvement and academics, there are benefits in increased student attendance, positive parent-child communication, improved student attitudes, and more parent-community support of the school (Rich, 1985). In spite of these clear advantages of parent involvement, all too frequently urban African-American families do not participate in school-improvement efforts. There are four reasons for this:

- Lack of teacher training on involving families
- Myth that African-American families do not care about education
- Parents' prior negative school experiences
- Prevalence of single-parent households

LACK OF TEACHER TRAINING

Few teachers undergo training on involving parents, especially minority parents. During the spring of 1991, a phone survey of 22 universities in the state of North Carolina revealed that none offered an undergraduate or graduate course on effective parental-involvement strategies. As a result of the survey and a demand by local educators, I established a summer institute for veteran educators through the Continuing Education and Extension program at the University of North Carolina at Charlotte.

The title of the summer institute was "Effective Parental Involvement and Parental Education Strategies for Educators." Myriad and diverse educators from as far as 60 miles away enrolled in the course. They included public-school teachers, school psychologists, administrators, guidance counselors, coordinators and counselors for dropout-prevention programs, case managers, social workers, and parents. The summer institute targeted specific topics and field experiences to reinforce those topics. There were visits to Chapter I Parent-Involvement Programs and visits to successful parent centers at nearby public schools. Visits and interviews were scheduled, with many programs effective in motivating African-American students (Reglin, 1993a). The specific topics covered in the summer institute need to be integrated in all inservice training programs for educators. These topics included

- Making Sense of Noninvolvement
- Single Parents' Noninvolvement

- Awareness, Action, and Reflection
- Urban African-American Alienation
- Urban African-American Involvement
- Dealing with Teachers' "Attitudes"
- Suggestions for Teachers
- Families as Self-Esteem "Builders" and Tutors
- School Administrators and Involvement
- Suggestions for School Administrators
- Parent Centers
- Home Visiting and Home Visitors Programs
- Interviews and Visits with Model Parental Involvement Programs

See Reglin (1993a) for detailed descriptions.

Fewer than 4 percent of teacher-education programs offer courses in parent involvement, even though 91 percent of teachers feel that the role of the parent as a school program supporter is important. Because of insufficient training, it is difficult for teachers to capitalize on the awesome power derived from good relations with urban African-American parents.

Teachers who want to involve African-American parents can find little material on how to establish such relations effectively. They often become frustrated by this paucity of information and transfer their frustration to other teachers (Chavkin, 1989). Yet teachers are expected by principals to be capable of working effectively with African-American parents.

MYTH THAT AFRICAN-AMERICAN PARENTS DO NOT CARE ABOUT EDUCATION

Second, the myth that urban African-American parents do not care about the education of their children hinders involvement. All parents care about their children's education and have a strong interest in being involved in the school (Williams & Chavkin, 1984). Often they are not invited to participate in planning where activities will take place or how much they will cost individual children. Involvement at school is limited for some because they do not have transportation. For a smaller group, their own problems are so pressing that they cannot focus on how their child is doing in school. To assist families in solving some of their family problems so that more parental effort can be devoted to school involvement, teachers should have access to the names, addresses, and phone numbers of community and government agencies with the resources to help. Agencies should be invited into the school to help work with students and parents.

It is important to listen carefully when conversing with African-American parents and students to find out whether they need the services of one of the identified agencies. School personnel should be prepared to provide them with the appropriate referral information, and teachers should feel free to request that an administrator, social worker, counselor, or school psychologist assist. Agencies that commonly provide services for African-American families include the following:

- Community health agencies
- Children's medical services
- Housing authority
- Teen parenting programs
- GED programs
- Adult literacy programs
- Private preschools and child care
- Subsidized child care
- Religious groups
- African-American civic organizations
- Diagnostic and learning resource systems
- Pre K-early elementary programs
- Head Start programs

PRIOR NEGATIVE SCHOOL EXPERIENCES

Third, because of their own negative experiences with school as students, some urban African-American parents do not believe the schools sincerely want to educate their children or involve them as partners. They see schools as favoring the children of middle-income and high-income families (Lewis, 1992). This perception causes the parents and family members to harbor negative feelings and a sense of powerlessness.

These parents are too distrustful of schools in general to help their local schools educate their children. Muriel Hamilton-Lee (1988) prescribed three solutions:

- getting parents involved in special activities such as the P.T.A. and school outings
- enlisting them in regular school affairs as assistant teachers or library aides
- incorporating them on planning and management teams.

Having parents involved and working with school professionals as colleagues and peers does a great deal to minimize the barriers between them. Empathy is critical in tearing down the barriers.

SINGLE-PARENT HOUSEHOLDS

Fourth, most urban African-American children are from single-parent families. Single-parent families' unique circumstances hinder effective involvement. Thirty percent of school-age children see their families dissolved by divorce (Carlson, 1990). Studies show that children from single-parent families are more likely to show behavioral problems such as absenteeism, tardiness, truancy, inefficient study habits at home, and disruptive classroom behavior.

The proportion of poor children living in female-headed households has risen sharply, from 24 percent in 1960 to 58 percent in 1990. For African-American children living in poverty, the increase was even more dramatic, from 29 percent in 1960 to 80 percent in 1990 (OERI, 1992). The trend is serious because a one-parent family's chances of ending up in poverty are six times as high as a two-parent family's.

Other problems also pervade one-parent families. Giving children autonomy too early (permissiveness) has negative effects on achievement. Dornbusch & Gray (1988) found that single parents mostly used permissive parenting styles as opposed to authoritarian parenting styles. Authoritarian parenting styles have a positive relationship with school performance. Authoritarian styles are characterized by high expectations, firm enforcement of rules, open communication between parent and child, and encouragement of the adolescent's individuality and independence (Chavkin, 1989).

IMPROVING COMMUNICATIONS WITH AFRICAN-AMERICAN PARENTS

Teachers cannot teach urban African-American children without being in constant contact with the parents. It is important to phone them at the beginning of the year and maintain constant contact as the year unfolds. An effort should be made to contact all parents, even those who may not want to hear from the school.

Teachers and administrators need to be encouraged to become members of the community. They should expect to attend most school and community functions so they can meet as many parents as possible. Even a smile and a brief conversation in the grocery store can do much to establish good parent-teacher relations. It should be routine to report good news about the child to the parent as well as any behaviors requiring improvement. Many urban African-American parents hear from teachers only when things are not going well. One parent told a teacher, "You never have anything good to say." One day the teacher sent a positive note home to the parent of a child who had been tardy 21 times. Would you believe? She was never tardy again.

It is imperative to acknowledge African-American parents who are making an extra effort. Prompt notes, phone calls, and verbal messages will let them know that their help is appreciated. A note or care package sent at Thanksgiving, Christmas, or Valentine's Day is an especially nice "thank you." Some teachers who use such techniques have had parents who kept notes from thankful teachers in a picture frame at the office desk or on the wall at home for many months.

The principal or assistant principal can be enlisted to acknowledge the contributions these parents are making through personal phone calls, memos, African-American newspapers, African-American radio stations, and at-school functions. This will translate into increased credibility in the African-American community. The next year, if there is a problem with some disgruntled parent who complains to other parents, the complaint will likely fall on deaf ears because the school staff has already established a positive reputation in dealing with African-American parents.

Teachers and administrators can conduct workshops for parents to introduce them to techniques they can use to reinforce classroom efforts. Parents should be given a chance to talk to one another at these workshops. They will get a lot of support from one another when they see how universal child-rearing problems are. Teachers can also write notes in students' homework books. Such notes might read, "Jamal did better in English today because of the help you gave him," or "I couldn't have managed the class party without your help."

When positive communications cause African-American parents to feel that they are part of the school team, the parents lose a lot of the anxiety remaining from their unpleasant associations with schools and teachers. Many of their own teachers were probably not as enlightened or supportive as the reader of this text is likely to be. These negative feelings from past unpleasant associations need to be overcome before anything else is attempted.

The starting point must be for teachers to establish positive communications with African-American parents early in the school year. At the beginning of the year, principals or other administrators should get the names of all teachers who want parent and/or family-member volunteers. Some teachers may feel that parents are more hindrance than help in the classroom and prefer to work alone, but they should make extra efforts to establish and maintain close relationships with the parents outside the classroom. Those who feel that parents are not interested in their children may need to work with or observe another teacher who has established good interactions with families. Teachers who want help from parents and/or family members should list the dates and times they will need volunteers. Letters or a newsletter can be sent to all families listing these requests. The model of "Parent/Family Help Letter" (see page 105) can be tailored to individual schools and mailed by the parent coordinator to the children's homes.

Some parents and/or family members will want or require letters mailed to employers to support their requests for time off from work to volunteer or attend activities at the school. Schools should be prepared to mail a letter to the parent's employer that is modeled on the "Employer Help Letter" (see page 106).

MOLDING FAMILY-FRIENDLY RELATIONSHIPS

From a policy perspective, the only way to bridge the gap between urban African-American parents and schools is to provide teachers with more time and opportunities to become familiar with their students and their students' home environments. Deliberate action can be taken to make the school family-friendly to parents. Many urban African-American families feel a sense of isolation, intimidation, and powerlessness about the schooling and education of their children.

In the education of African-American children, the high visibility of their parents is a plus. For example, during one of my workshops a teacher said, "One of my African-American students disrupted the class. After calling home and talking to both parents, I was elated with the results. He no longer misbehaved in class and his improved behavior made a positive impact upon his class work."

Two good reasons why the student's conduct improved are, first, that his parents threatened to sit in class with him and, second, that both African-American parents wanted him to have what neither of them received—a high school diploma. This incident indicates the importance of contacting African-American families and promoting family-friendly connections.

Given the fact that a large number of African-American parents cannot come to the school, parent support at home is a much more realistic possibility for them. There are some parents who cannot provide much support to their children and even less to the school. For this small percentage of parents the school will have to assume greater responsibility for their children.

Educators should recognize that they need the help of urban African-American parents in educating their children. They can enlist their support by going into African-American communities and expressing their conviction that it takes the entire village to educate kids properly. A user-friendly plan for parent support needs to be developed and closely monitored. This plan has to include a variety of school-involvement strategies.

There are two keys to this plan. One is to communicate clearly to the parents just what you would like them to do. The other is to ensure the implementation of diverse school involvement strategies that focus on parents' strengths and interests as much as feasible. At the same time, it is important to keep in mind that parents are not—and should not be expected to be—teachers.

African-American parent support does not preclude some of the more traditional types of parental participation. There are always those who can and want to have direct involvement with the schools. These individuals can be very helpful in assisting teachers in tutoring students or preparing lessons. However, teachers should never lose sight of the major goal of African-American parental support: to help increase student achievement.

All parent-support activities must be as directly related to that goal as much as possible. Educators should select as many as possible of the 15 "Family-Friendly Activities" (see page 107) for inclusion in the school-parent support plan.

IMPROVING HOME-SCHOOL-COMMUNITY CONNECTIONS

School administrators and teachers must be creative in developing and implementing programs that promote African-American parent involvement. For example, Briggs Middle School in Springfield, Oregon, hired a parent educator and a therapist to work directly with parents of children at risk (Hart, 1988). They contacted 75 parents, 10 of whom completed the training curriculum for parent educators.

A program developed by the Center for Research on Elementary and Middle Schools (1989) enabled teachers to involve African-American parents in their children's education in math, science, and social studies. The TIPS (Teachers Involve Parents in Schoolwork) program consists of guidelines and materials that any school or district can adapt to its own curriculum objectives. It calls for parents to help their children with math and science homework and to make presentations in social studies classes.

The De Kalb County School System in Georgia used signed contracts to underscore the importance of parent involvement. The contract, which is signed by the student and the teacher, commits the parent to talking about school daily, attending teacher-parent conferences, monitoring television viewing, and encouraging good study habits. In turn, the teacher agrees to provide motivating and interesting experiences in the classroom, explain the grading system, provide homework, and so forth. The district holds the signing at the beginning of each school year.

Educators must be innovative in promoting the home-school-community connections. Research and my personal experience have identified 10 proven home-school-community connections. These school-initiated strategies are important to increase the involvement of urban African-American families in the public-school education process and to enhance the successes of the students. However, the strategies will not be effective if they are not supported by the community. "Ten School-Initiated Strategies for Improving Community Involvement" (see pages 108-109) specifies school and community roles.

RECRUITING MALE TEACHERS, MENTORS, AND GUEST SPEAKERS

Research and my personal experience suggest that there is an urgent need for communities to respond to the pleas for help from teachers and failing African-American students. First, the community needs to encourage talented African-American high-school students to pursue professions as public-school teachers. Second, the community needs to become a source of positive male mentors and male guest speakers.

If the current demographic trends continue, the number of African-American teachers will actually decline (Daniels, 1989). While we can do a better job of preparing all ethnic groups for classroom roles, there must be more visible African-American teachers, especially African-American male teachers, as positive mentors and guest speakers in the classroom.

Eighty-three percent of elementary-school teachers are women and only 0.2 percent are African-American men. Forty-six percent of secondary teachers are women and only 3.2 percent are men. Only 1.2 percent of all teachers are African-American men. The predominance of women in elementary and secondary education results in African-American male students' disproportionate reliance on their peer groups for learning values and appropriate behavior (Kunjufu, 1984).

Because it will take time to attract more African-American male teachers to the teaching profession, teachers in the classroom should work with the African-American communities and the African-American churches to get more positive African-American male mentors and male guest speakers. The mentors and guest speakers can come into the classroom to tell their stories. In cases where African-American males are simply not available for whatever reason, community groups should direct interested, positive, understanding males of any ethnic group as acceptable substitutes.

Numerous studies and experiences concur that classrooms are enriched by links with their communities. There are valuable and interesting people in many communities who, if invited, will share their experiences with students. The best sources of mentors and guest speakers may be found in local businesses and local churches. Teachers can work with the urban African-American community to get the community to assist in the four ways described in "Supporting Schools' Needs for Positive Role Models" (see page 110).

IMPLICATIONS

In 1991 the U.S. Department of Education released *America 2000: An Education Strategy*, a report that outlined some important goals to be met by the year 2000 (U.S. Department of Education, 1991). *America 2000* pointed out the following facts:

(1) Too many of our children do not have the kind of family that serves as their protector, advocate, and moral anchor.

(2) For too many children, their neighborhoods are a place of menace, the street a place of violence.

(3) Too many children arrive at school hungry, dirty, and frightened.

(4) Too many children start school not ready to meet the challenges of learning.

A significant number of the children targeted in *America 2000* are urban African-American students. The children's home environments and cultural backgrounds have resulted in development at odds with the mainstream system. They are failing or at risk of failing in the traditional educational system. The children enter school with a distinct educational disadvantage. Some behave according to the expectations of the home, which may be radically different from those of the school. They enter the school unprepared to "bridge the social and cultural gap between home and school" (Comer, 1987).

Many urban African-American communities are hard put to find the resources to help such children. The communities are plagued by violence, drug abuse, teenage pregnancy, racism, and other behaviors and attitudes that are detrimental to human health, equity, and achievement (Duttweiler & Mutchler, 1990). African-American children living under such conditions are too often neglected by parents, churches, social service agencies, and health services. Yet we know that school achievement is affected by all facets of a child's life: safety, nutrition, physical well-being, and mental health (Pollard, 1990).

Teachers alone cannot handle the problems of underachieving African-American students. Such problems must become the collective interest of the state departments of education, schools, African-American families, African-American communities, and the majority communities. Building partnerships among these important elements is essential.

A good lead to follow is the 1989 Kentucky Supreme Court ruling that declared the Kentucky school system unconstitutional. The Kentucky Legislature passed the Education Reform Act. One of the major strategies of the act was to remove impediments to learning. To that end, 206 Family Resource and Youth Service Centers have thus far been funded to enable schools to link students and their families to social and health service agencies and other community resources (Kentucky Department of Education, 1992).

Research consistently finds that African-American parent involvement has a high positive correlation with African-American children's achievement. African-American parents are their children's first and most important teachers. To perform adequately in school, the children must reside in a home and community environment that complements the values of the school. Parent training is important in this effort (Taylor, 1991). Schools must recognize that they need the help of African-American parents in educating their children. Schools need to be innovative in reaching out to African-American parents and encouraging their involvement.

From a policy perspective, the only way to bridge the gap between African-American parents and schools is to provide teachers with more time to become familiar with their students and their students' home environment. More deliberate action needs to be taken to make the school family-friendly to parents.

Lastly, principals and public-school staff-development directors have a significant responsibility. Training of teachers in the area of parent and community involvement is weak. Few teachers undergo any training on this issue at all, and they are especially lacking in background on involving urban African-American parents. Training based on the strategies mentioned in this chapter will restructure schools and universities to foster better African-American parent involvement.

PARENT/FAMILY HELP LETTER MODEL

[YOUR SCHOOL'S LETTERHEAD]

[Date]

Dear Parent/Family Member:

We are asking for your help with our school activities. We know your time is valuable, so any minutes or hours you can give us will be greatly appreciated. You can help with some of the following tasks. Some require your help at school. Others can be done at home.

Please check the ways you are willing to assist us.

I prefer to help out _____ in the classroom _____ at home.

Which activities can you assist us with?

Classroom activities

_____ Reading to students
_____ Helping in our parent center
_____ Working as a tutor
_____ Making bulletin boards
_____ Counseling students
_____ Helping with math
_____ Helping with writing
_____ Helping with computer activities
_____ Accompanying field trips
_____ Answering the office phone

At-home activities

_____ Working on school committees
_____ Checking spelling
_____ Checking papers
_____ Coordinating involvement from other parents

Any other activities you would like to help with? _____

Suggestions? _____

Comments? _____

What time would you be available to help?

_____ mornings _____ afternoons _____ weekends _____ nights

Do you want us to send a letter to your employer requesting that you be given time off to help in the school and to visit the school for conferences? _____ yes _____ no

If "yes," please provide employer's name and address: _____

_____

Parent's Name _____ Phone _____

Child's/Children's names and teachers: _____

_____   _____

(Signed)   The Principal

EMPLOYER HELP LETTER MODEL

[YOUR SCHOOL'S LETTERHEAD]

[Date]

Dear Employer:

In your position, you know the value of teamwork. When families and educators work together, they make an effective partnership that will benefit families, children, the school, and our local businesses. An important goal at our school is to get all parents involved productively in their children's education.

We need your help to achieve our goal. Your employee(s)

[name(s)] _____
generously offered to help us here at school if occasional time off from work can be arranged that is convenient with work schedules and demands.

We would be very grateful for your cooperation in providing such time off as is needed for volunteer work in the school and school conferences. By supporting a family's involvement in its children's education, you will be strengthening the home-school-community connection, employee productivity, and employee morale.

We thank you in advance for honoring these occasional requests from the school or the employee. We also extend to you a warm invitation to visit us and learn about the programs we are initiating to involve families and the community in our school.

Your cooperation confirms that you are a valued supporter of our school.

Sincerely,

(signed) Principal/Teacher

FAMILY-FRIENDLY ACTIVITIES

1. Vary the meeting times of Open House. Hold some in the afternoon, some at night.

2. Invite some of the African-American parents to sample the school lunch once a month. Seat them with the principal, a teacher, and several selected students.

3. Hold a Senior Citizens Day at the school, inviting grandparents and older friends of the school. Provide transportation.

4. Send home Happy Grams—good news notes about accomplishments and achievements.

5. Have students interview their parents and grandparents about how life has changed since childhood.

6. Encourage parents to praise their children's successes.

7. Conduct surveys and provide parents with research on such things as average hours of sleep per night by grade, average hours devoted to homework, television viewing, etc.

8. Reward parents for their involvement. Coordinate a Parents' Breakfast or a recognition certificate to award at the end of the year.

9. Seek out the African-American parents who never participate. Sometimes these parents feel inadequate or timid and simply need to be encouraged and needed.

10. Give an assignment that requires the children to ask their parents questions.

11. Ask parents to get their children to talk each day about what they did in class.

12. Ask parents to watch a specific television program with their children and to discuss the show afterward.

13. Ask parents to sign homework to ensure its completion.

14. Ask parents to let the teacher know when there are events at home that may affect the children's performance at school. Such events could include a new sibling or illness of a family member.

15. Guide families into modeling an active interest in learning (e.g., reading and discussing current events, going to the library, talking about experiences and what family members have learned from them).

Ten School-Initiated Strategies for Improving Community Involvement

1. The initial thrust by schools to get some African-American parents involved might have to be social; once families are involved with the schools, the staff should work towards increased involvement (Comer, 1987). The community can assist by providing facilities (recreation centers, church meeting rooms, employers' meeting rooms, etc.), transportation, and publicity to support this endeavor.

2. The school facilities (e.g., theater, meeting room, gymnasium, etc.) should be open for families' use after school hours. The community can help by supplying volunteers to work in the facilities and by encouraging the families to use them.

3. Schools can work with social service or counseling agencies to establish support groups for children from divorced or separated families to help these young people cope with their problems. Churches may have similar child-support groups. They might also have well-established adult-support groups. Examples are single-parent groups, noncustodial-parent groups, and grandparent groups. Leaders or members of these groups can assist with the school support groups.

4. Schools can turn parents into teachers by creating learning activities that parents can use at home with their children. The activities should reinforce classroom instruction. They should be brief and fun. Examples include brain teasers and puzzles. Churches, Optimist Clubs, 100 Black Men Organizations, National Association for the Advancement of Colored People (NAACP), African-American Fraternities, and African-American Sororities can be strong advocates for this initiative. They should be proactive in marketing this initiative verbally and through the organizations' literature.

5. Family members enjoy seeing their children on stage performing in plays or participating in sports such as basketball or football. Schools should phone parents and encourage them to come and see their children perform. Hold a small business meeting, but limit the meeting to about 20 minutes. Have the meeting at the beginning of the school activity. The community should allow the school to use community facilities at little or no cost to the school. The community should encourage high attendance by community members at all school events. Local African-American radio stations and newspapers can assist with publicity.

6. Schools can set aside specified times for school conferences. Teachers at each school who succeed in drawing in the highest percentage of their students' parents for a conference can be rewarded, perhaps with a day off. Employers in business and industry should be encouraged to allow parents time off from work to attend the conferences (see "Employer Help Letter Model" on page 106).

7. Schools can disseminate information about school events through newsletters and calendars. These should be mailed to the homes or places in the communities that families visit frequently, such as grocery stores or recreation centers, where they can be displayed in highly visible locations. The local newspapers might be asked to print all or parts of the newsletters and calendars in their pages.

8. Schools can target popular predominantly African-American radio stations and newspapers. Ask popular radio stations for weekly radio spots so that educators or parents or family members can talk about the activities at school. The media can be supportive.

9. Schools can employ family members as teacher aides, teacher assistants, clerical workers, custodians, and substitute teachers within the schools. A formal request to business and industries might result in a flexible work schedule for families who work in these school positions.

10. Schools could have regular contests for students to create or complete projects related to subjects they are currently studying. Parents should be asked to visit the school once a month to judge the projects. Student winners should receive prizes—monetary, if possible—and parent judges could also receive prizes based on the number of times they participate in the program. Community organizations and businesses can be approached to provide the prizes and encourage the participation of the parent judges.

SUPPORTING SCHOOLS' NEEDS FOR POSITIVE ROLE MODELS

1. Male physicians, corporate managers, dentists, policemen, ministers, and military officers who are African-American or of any other ethnic group can be involved with the public schools as mentors and guest speakers. They can be invited to spend from 30 minutes of a lunch hour to four hours a day in the classroom.

2. Local colleges and universities may be able to provide African-American and other ethnic-group male mentors and guest speakers who are university professors, staff personnel, or college students.

3. Local churches may also be able to provide mentors and guest speakers, either African-American or from other ethnic groups. African-American churches can be rich resources, as ministers realize the importance of the current need and can promote participation with local schools among neighborhoods and organizations.

4. When suitable role models and mentors have been targeted, schools should work with local communities to establish community- and church-based mentor programs that focus on four objectives: attendance, academic achievement, social skills (especially those appropriate for today's males), and appropriate behavior for school life.

ACTIVITIES FOR READERS OF CHAPTER FOUR

1. What is meant by schools being "family-friendly"? Review the 15 "Family-Friendly Activities" (see page 107). How many are in your school's parent-support plan? Identify any activities that are not in the plan but that you feel should be included. Describe a strategy that you could use to ensure that the missing activities are included in your school's parent-support plan.

2. Male mentors are very effective in working with underachieving urban African-American male students. List all viable sources of African-American male mentors in your community. Identify the African-American male students in your class or school who require the help of mentors. Develop a five-page proposal for submission to an organization that could be a potential source of mentors. At a minimum, your proposal should deal with the following issues:

   a. How mentors will be trained in mentoring procedures

   b. How mentors will be matched to students

   c. The mentors' specific responsibilities

   d. The number of times the mentors will be expected to meet with the students each month

   e. The kind of background information on students' hobbies, interests, classroom behavior, classroom academic performance, family history, etc., that will be provided to the mentors

   f. The nature and frequency of the feedback to the teacher that each mentor will be expected to provide

SUGGESTED READINGS FOR CHAPTER FOUR

Kentucky Department of Education. (1992, September). Building a sense of community. *EdNews Special Section.*

Comer, J. (1987). New Haven's school-community connection. *Educational Leadership,* 44(6), 13-16.

Comer, J. (1988). Educating poor and minority children. *Scientific American,* 259(5), 42-48.

Kunjufu, J. (1984). *Developing positive self-images and discipline in Black children.* Chicago: African-American Images.

Murphy, J. (1993). What's in? What's out? American education in the nineties. *Phi Delta Kappan,* 74(8), 641-645.

Reglin, G.L. (1993). *At-risk "parent and family" involvement: Strategies for low-income families and African-American families of unmotivated and underachieving students.* Springfield, IL: Charles C. Thomas, Publisher.

CONCLUSION

Who succeeds in school? Who fails? The answer is well documented by research. Children from low-income homes are more likely to fail than those from middle- and high-income homes. Urban African-Americans are more likely to fail. African-American students start school with high expectations and a strong desire to do well, but something happens along the way to destroy their expectations and desire. Many lose interest in school and become withdrawn, rebellious, and defiant.

Sometimes capable students who are respected by their fellow community members fail to keep up with the other students once they enter the classroom. A label of "failure" is attached by school and society—a label that follows them throughout their academic and adult lives. All children can learn and achieve success in school. None should be labeled a likely failure because of social, economic, or cultural considerations.

To promote the cognitive and academic development of urban African-American public-school children, teaching practices in the public schools have to be restructured. Restructuring means implementing sensitive instruction and behaviors supportive of African-American children's achievement in classrooms. No longer can the sole focus of the classroom be on teaching content and teaching children as though they were from the same cultural background. Lecture, seat work, and discussion must cease to be the dominant teaching strategy. Teachers should teach the whole child.

To teach the whole child effectively, teachers will need training in cooperative learning, learning-styles instruction, the use of technology, team teaching, climate enhancing, cross-age tutoring strategies, and peer-tutoring strategies. Instructional techniques to combat feelings of victimization and to build self-esteem will need to be built into the teaching repertoire. Social, emotional, physical, and academic growth and development of children are inextricably linked. Teachers will need to be taught how to deal with all dimensions of children in the school. Coursework and inservice experiences should be placed within a cultural context.

Teaching urban African-American children presents an important challenge. It involves committed people preparing the students in their care with the knowledge, skills, and values that will aid them in living a fulfilling life, which even in the best of times is not an easy task. It becomes even more difficult in situations where students lack hope.

Underachieving African-American students are often sending a powerful message to teachers: "I do not care what you know until I know that you care." Teachers must be persuaded that they need to establish a caring relationship with the students. Teaching is a highly personal business. Teachers who respond mechanically and impersonally are not likely to be creative and to establish good rapport with African-American students. Mechanical, inflexible teachers unintentionally send disinviting messages.

113

Classrooms do not exist in isolation. Positive interactions will have to be initiated with African-American students outside classrooms. What happens to African-American students on the way to school, in the hallway, cafeteria, gymnasium, and on the playground affects the way they perform in classrooms. Teachers can be advocates for their African-American students, committed to fighting the societal conditions that economically and emotionally limit students' chances of achieving success in school.

Education does not begin and end at the schoolhouse door. School occupies only nine percent of children's lives, and the rest is spent outside of school (Murphy, 1993). Uncles, aunts, cousins, parents, churches, social welfare organizations, peers, recreational centers, outdoor basketball courts, and many other social and cultural agents all play major roles in shaping the lives of many African-American students, and educators need to become knowledgeable about these influences. They should pursue experiences that lead them to interact with the influences that occupy the other 91 percent of the students' lives.

African-American youth must be encouraged—not discouraged. Negative expectations, low standards, competition, and double standards all promote discouragement and are often alienating to underachieving African-American youth. Most African-American students have not learned very much because teachers have not pushed them hard enough. Teachers must maintain high standards, be creative, and challenge students at every opportunity.

Working effectively with parents is imperative. Parents must be informed of the importance of good family values, involvement, and participation in their children's education. Clark (1992) confirmed the importance of family values in a study that examined the attitudes of low-income minority families. The families who placed importance on family values produced more students who were near the top of their class. Schools must include parents at times other than when their children are in trouble. Comer (1986) indicated that the presence of African-American parents and the support they offer decrease conflict and apathy in the school.

More innovative strategies supporting instruction and behaviors that are sensitive to ethnic minorities, especially African-Americans—beyond those listed throughout the text—will enhance the achievement of minorities. The number of strategies is limited only by the imagination, determination, and energy of teachers and school administrators.

Selected Bibliography

Albert, L. (1990). *Cooperative discipline: Classroom management that promotes self-esteem.* Circle Pines, MN: American Guidance Service.

Ascher, C. (1992). School programs for African-American males...and females. *Phi Delta Kappan,* 73(10), 777-782.

Banks, J. (1989). Teacher education and students of color: Conceptualizing the problem. Paper presented at the Annual Meeting of the American Educational Research Association.

Banks, J.A. (1993a). Multicultural education: Development, dimensions, and challenges. *Phi Delta Kappan,* 75(1), 22-28.

Banks, J.A. (1993b). The canon debate, knowledge construction, and multicultural education. *Educational Researcher,* 22(5), 4-14.

Bennett, C. (1990). *Comprehensive multicultural education.* Boston, MA: Allyn & Bacon.

Brigman, G. (1993). Promoting students' self-discipline by teaching social skills and learning skills. *The National Dropout Prevention Newsletter,* 6(4), 7.

Canfield, J. (1990). Improving students' self-esteem. *Educational Leadership,* 48(1), 48-50.

Carlson, C.I. (1990). Best practices in working with single-parent and stepparent family systems. In Thomas, A., and Grimes, J.: *Best practices in school psychology—II.* Washington, DC: National Association of School Psychologists.

Center for Research on Elementary and Middle Schools (1989). Parent involvement program in middle schools helps students gain awareness and knowledge of artists and paintings. CREMS, p. 7-9.

Chavkin, N.F. (1989). Debunking the myth about minority parents. *Educational Horizons,* 67(4), 119-123.

Clark, B. (1992). *Growing up gifted: Developing the potential of children at home and school* (4th ed.). New York: Merrill/Macmillan.

Comer, J. (1987a). Educating poor and minority children. *Scientific American,* 259(5), 42-48.

Comer, J. (1987b). New Haven's school-community connection. *Educational Leadership,* 44(6), 13-16.

Comer, J. (1991). Understanding students at risk. Report to the Second Annual Conference on youth at Risk. Savannah, GA: Georgia Southern University.

Commission on Minority Participation in Education and American Life. (1988). *One-third of a nation.* Washington, DC: The American Council on Education.

Council of Chief State School Officers. (1987). *Children at risk: The work of the states.* Washington, DC: Council of Chief State School Officers.

Cummins, B.M. (1986). The context of education for minority students: An overview. *American Journal of Education, 29,* 27-57.

Daniels, L.A. (1989). Many minority teachers plan to quit, poll finds. *New York Times,* p. B-13.

Delpit, L.D. (1988). The silenced dialogue: Power and pedagogy in educating other people's children. *Harvard Educational Review, 58*(3), 280-298.

Dornbusch, S.M., & Gray, K.D. (1988). Single-parent families. In Dornbusch, S.M. and Strober, M.H.: *Feminism, children, and the new families.* New York: Guilford Press, 274-296.

Duttweiler, P.C., & Mutchler, S.E. (1990). *Organizing the educational system for excellence: Harnessing the energy of people.* Austin, TX: Southwest Educational Development Laboratory.

Edmonds, R. (1979). Some schools work and more can. *Social Policy, 9*(5), 28-32.

Edwards, P.A., & Young, L.S. (1992). Beyond parents: Family, community, and school involvement. *Phi Delta Kappan, 74*(1), 72-80.

Eisner, E.W. (1985). *The educational imagination: On the design and evaluation of school programs.* New York: Macmillan.

Elias, M.J., & Tobias, S.E. (1990). *Problem solving/decision making for social and academic success.* Washington, DC: National Education Association.

Ellis, S.S., & Whalen, S.F. (1992). Keys to cooperative learning: 35 ways to keep kids responsible, challenged, and most of all cooperative. *Instructor, 101*(6), 34-37.

Emmer, E., Evertson, C., & Anderson L. (1980). Effective classroom management at the beginning of the school year. *Elementary School Journal, 80*(5), 219-231.

Evertson, C., Anderson, L., & Brophy, J.E. (1980). Relationship between classroom behaviors and student outcomes in junior high mathematics and English classes. *American Educational Research Journal, 17*(1), 43-60.

Fisher, R., & Ury, W. (1983). *Getting to yes: Negotiating agreements without giving in.* New York: Penguin Books.

Garton, S. (1984). Improving instruction for the economically disadvantaged students. *NASSP Bulletin, 68*(472), 91-96.

Gay, G. (1988). Redesigning relevant curricula for diverse learners. *Education and Urban Society, 2*(4), 327-340.

Good, T.L., & Brophy, J.E. (1991). *Looking in classrooms.* New York: HarperCollins.

Goodlad, J.I. (1984). Introduction: The uncommon common school. *Education and Urban Society, 16*(3), 243-252.

Hale-Benson, J.E. (1986). *Black children: Their roots, culture, and learning styles.* Baltimore: Johns Hopkins Press.

Hamilton-Lee, M. (1988). Home-school partnerhips: The school development model. Paper presented at the Annual Convention of the American Psychological Association.

Hart, T.E. (1988). *Involving parents in the education of their children.* Eugene, OR: Oregon School Study Council.

Honing, B. (1990). High standards and great expectations: The foundations for student achievement. *The Early Adolescence,* 49(4), 8-11.

Irvine, J.J. (1990). *Black students and school failure: Policies, practices, and prescriptions.* New York: Prager.

Jenks, C.L (1988). A generic model of organizational inquiry for educational design. In *The redesign of education: A collection of papers concerned with comprehensive educational reform.* San Francisco, CA: Far West Laboratory.

Johnson, D.W., Johnson, R., & Holubec, E.J. (1988). *Cooperation in the classroom.* Edina, MN.: Interaction Books.

Johnson, J. (1990). *Introduction to the foundations of American education.* Boston: Allyn & Bacon.

Johnson, W., & Packer, G. (1987). *Workforce 2000: Work and workers for the twenty-first century.* Indianapolis: Hudson Institute.

Kentucky Department of Education. (1992, September). Building a sense of community. *EdNews Special Section.*

Knapp, M.S., Turnbull, B.J., & Shields. (1990). New directions for educating the children of poverty. *Educational Leadership,* 48(1), 4-8.

Kunjufu, J. (1984). *Developing positive self-images and discipline in Black children.* Chicago: African-American Images.

Lewis, D. (1992). *The forgotten factor in school success: The family.* Washington, DC: Home and School Institute.

Majors, R., & Billson, J. (1992). *Cool pose: The dilemmas of Black manhood in America.* New York: Lexington Books.

Marable, M. (1993, September 9). Facing reality of a multicultural society. *The Charlotte Post,* p. 5A.

Melear, C.T., & Pitchford, F. (1992). *African-American science student learning style.* (ERIC Document Reproduction Service No. ED 314 158).

Michelson, R.A. (1990). The attitude-achievement paradox among Black adolescents. *Sociology of Education,* 63(10), 44-61.

Murphy, J. (1993). What's in? What's out? American education in the nineties. *Phi Delta Kappan.* 74(8), 641-645.

Nicklos, L.B., & Brown, W.S. (1989). Recruiting minorities into the teaching profession: An educational imperative. *Educational Horizons, 67*(4), 145-149.

O'Connor, T. (1989). Cultural voice and strategies for multicultural education. *Journal of Education, 171*(2), 57-74.

OERI. (1992). *Digest of educational statistics.* Washington, DC: National Center for Education Statistics, Office of Educational Research and Improvement, U.S. Department of Education.

Ogbu, J. (1990). Minority education in comparative perspective. *Journal of Negro Education, 59*(1), 46-49.

Ogbu, J.U. (1992). Understanding cultural differences and school learning. *Educational Libraries, 16*(3), 7-11.

Owens, I.L. (1993). Understanding the young Black male client in SAPs. *Student Assistance Journal, 6*(3), 20-34.

Pollard, J. (1990, May). School-linked services: So that schools can educate and children can learn. *INSIGHTS on Educational Policy and Practice* (Number 20). Austin, TX: Southwest Educational Development Laboratory.

Prawat, R.S. (1985). Affective versus cognitive goal orientations in elementary teachers. *American Educational Research Journal, 22*(4), 587-604.

Prince, T. (1990). *Community and service projects at Morehouse College targeted to at-risk youth.* Unpublished Manuscript. Morehouse College Counseling Center, p. 3.

Quality Education for Minorities Project. (1990). *Education that works: An action plan for the education of minorities.* (ERIC Document Reproduction Service No. ED 316 626).

Ravitch, A. (1991). A culture in common. *Educational Leadership, 49*(4), 8-11.

Reglin, G.L. (1990). A model program for educating at-risk students. *Technological Horizons in Education Journal, 17*(6), 65-67.

Reglin, G.L. (1993a). *Motivating low-achieving students: A special focus on unmotivated and underachieving African-American students.* Springfield, IL.: Charles C. Thomas, Publisher.

Reglin, G.L. (1993b). *At-risk "parent and family" involvement: Strategies for low-income families and African-American families of unmotivated and underachieving students.* Springfield, IL: Charles C. Thomas, Publisher.

Reglin, G.L., & Harris, S. (1991). *Effectively addressing the needs of middle school and high school at-risk Black males in solving the problems of youth at-risk.* Lancaster, PA: Technomic.

Rich, D. (1985). *The forgotten factor in school success: The family.* Washington, DC: The Home and School.

Rubalcava, D. (1991). Understanding students at risk. *Thresholds in Education, 16*(2), 5.

Saracho, O.N., & Gerstl, C.K. (1992). Learning differences among at-risk minority students. In Waxman, H.C., Felix, J.E., Anderson, L.E., and Baptiste, H.P.: *Students at risk in at-risk schools.* Newbury Park, CA: Corwin Press, pp. 105-135.

Shade, J.R. (1989). *Culture, style, and the education process.* Springfield, IL: Charles C. Thomas Publisher.

Slavin, R.A. (1983). *Cooperative learning.* New York: Longman.

Taylor, A.R. (1991). Social competence and the early school transition. *Education and Urban Society,* 24(1), 15-26.

Tyrrell, R. (1990). What teachers say about cooperative learning. *Middle School Journal,* 10(2), 16-19.

Uchitelle, S., Bartz, D., & Hillman, L. (1989). Strategies for reducing suspensions. *Urban Education,* 24(2), 163-176.

U.S. Bureau of the Census. (1992). *Statistical abstract of the United States (112th ed.).* Washington, DC: U.S. Government Printing Office.

U.S. Department of Education. (1991). *America 2000: An education strategy.* Washington, DC: U.S. Department of Education.

Valverde, L.A. (1993). Philosophy of student acculturation. *Education and Urban Society,* 25(3), 246-253.

Walberg, H.J. (1984). Improving the productivity of American schools. *Educational Leadership,* 41(8), 19-27.

Wampler, F. (1993). Peer mediation for a new generation. *The National Dropout Prevention Newsletter,* 6(4), 4-5.

White-Hood, M. (1990). Unforgettable: The Black male student in our schools. *Early Adolescence,* 5(2), 11-12.

Wiley, E. (1990). Interview with Dr. Richard Majors, psychologist at University of Wisconsin–Eau Claire. *Black Issues in Higher Education,* 7(19), 1, 6-7.

Williams, D.L., & Chavkin, N.F. (1984). Final report of the parent involvement in education project. Washington, D.C.: National Institute of Education.

Wilson, S. (1992). Cooperative learning shows staying power. *Update,* 34(3), 2-3.

Wright, W.J. (1991). The endangered Black male child. *Educational Leadership,* 49(4), 14-16.

About *Achievement for African-American Student* and the National Educational Service

The mission of the National Educational Service is to help create environments in which **all** children and youth will succeed. *Achievement for African-American Students* is just one of many resources and staff development opportunities we provide that focus on building a **Community Circle of Caring™**. If you have any questions, comments, articles, manuscripts, or youth art you would like us to consider for publication, please contact us at the address below.

Staff Development Opportunities Include:

Integrating Technology Effectively
Improving Schools through Quality Leadership
Creating Professional Learning Communities
Building Cultural Bridges
Discipline with Dignity
Ensuring Safe Schools
Managing Disruptive Behavior
Reclaiming Youth At Risk
Working with Today's Families

National Educational Service
1252 Loesch Road
Bloomington, IN 47404
(812) 336-7700
(888) 763-9045 (toll free)
FAX (812) 336-7790
e-mail: nes@nesonline.com
www.nesonline.com

NEED MORE COPIES OR ADDITIONAL RESOURCES ON THIS TOPIC?

Need more copies of this book? Want your own copy? Need additional resources on this topic? If so, you can order additional materials by using this form or by calling us toll free at (888) 763-9045 or (812) 336-7700. Or you can order by FAX at (812) 336-7790.

Preview any resource for 30 days without obligation. If you are not completely satisfied, simply return it within 30 days of receiving it and owe nothing.

Title	Price*	Quantity	Total
Achievement for African-American Students: Strategies for the Diverse Classroom	$ 19.95		
From Rage to Hope: Strategies for Reclaiming Black and Hispanic Students	19.95		
Teaching in the Diverse Classroom: Learner-Centered Activities That Work	19.95		
Anger Management for Youth: Stemming Aggression and Violence	22.95		
Safe Schools: A Handbook for Violence Prevention	25.00		
Dealing with Youth Violence: What Schools and Communities Need to Know	18.95		
Containing Crisis: A Guide for Managing School Emergencies	19.95		
Breaking the Cycle of Violence (2-video set and Leader's Guide)	325.00		
Effective Strategies for Teaching Minority Students	16.95		
What Do I Do When...? How to Achieve Discipline with Dignity in the Classroom	21.95		
As Tough as Necessary (4-video set and Leader's Guide)	495.00		
Building Cultural Bridges (50-lesson curriculum, grades 7–12)	97.00		
Please add $3 handling and 5% of sales for regular domestic shipments within continental U.S.; or $5 handling and 7% of sales for special and/or non-domestic shipments.			

*Prices subject to change without notice   **TOTAL**_____

❏ Check enclosed   ❏ Please bill me (P.O. #_____)

❏ Money Order   ❏ VISA, MasterCard, Discover, or American Express

Credit Card No._____ Exp. Date _____

Cardholder Signature_____

SHIP TO:

Name_____ Title _____

Organization _____

Address_____

City_____ State_____ ZIP_____

Phone_____ FAX _____

National Educational Service
1252 Loesch Road
Bloomington, IN 47404
(812) 336-7700 • (888) 763-9045 (toll free)
FAX (812) 336-7790
e-mail: nes@nesonline.com • www.nesonline.com